SIMPLE:

UNDERSTANDING

REVELATION

JEFF MEYERS

Simple: Understanding Revelation

Jeff Meyers

© Copyright 2011, Jeffrey W. Meyers

ISBN-978-0-9846852-4-0

Table of Contents

Acknowledgement(s)

To any and all who have ever written a book, this is the most frightening part of the process. Why? What if I leave someone out or do not recognize someone who should have been? If by chance you are one of those, please let me know and I will include you in the 2nd printing!

First and foremost I must acknowledge my wife, Traci. Though I preached and wrote the material, there were many hours of discussion "behind the scenes." She not only challenged me to clarify and communicate but to think as well. Traci always sharpens my thinking in regard to Biblical passages, but no more so than in the book of Revelation.

Second, I must thank and acknowledge the wonderful people of the First Baptist Church of Conyers Georgia. Four years ago the Lord brought us together in a unique and special "pastor-church" relationship. May the fun never end and may we enjoy "changing the world, starting in Conyers, Georgia."

Third, I must acknowledge the ministerial and support staff of FBCC without whom this project would have never gotten off the ground much less become print material. During our series through Revelation you gave suggestions, made videos, tweaked, and cheered me to the finish line. It is a privilege to serve with all of you. Finally, I must thank those behind the madness. Yes, if were not for these four you would not have this book in your hands. To Bess Stewart and Edith Bowie who caught comma and syntax errors, not to mention a few misstatements or mistakes. Also, Jodi

5

Bailey, my editor. Originally, the content of this book was a series of sermons. And well, to be honest with you, sermons do not read well. Jodi was able to take the sermons that Bess had transcribed and Edith had edited and she turned them into the book you are reading today. Additionally, Becky Wilson is responsible for the layout and all the prep work that was necessary for the printing to take place – you guys make me look good, thanks!

Preface

This is not the book I would have written. However, I learned long ago that communication is not what someone says but what others hear. If I were going to write a book or commentary on the book of Revelation that I would want to, you would have no interest in reading it. It would be long and detailed. It would chase an endless stream of "theological rabbits." The footnotes would comprise over half of every page. Honestly, if I penned that book as many people as have read my dissertation would read it; I think it's up to 4 now.

Thankfully, for your sake, this book is not that book. This book is derived from a series that I preached through the book of Revelation in the summer of 2011 at FBCC. Because I have taught and preached through Revelation frequently, I knew that there were certain topics and characters that needed to be addressed from the beginning. In other words, starting at chapter 1 and going straight through to chapter 22 is not necessarily the best way to communicate the content of Revelation from a "sermonic" perspective. Therefore, we "borrowed" a page from George Lucas and the Star Wars saga.

What did we borrow? We started in the middle of the story and not at the beginning. So, as you turn the page you will find the beginning in chapter 11 and at the end you will be in chapter 7; when you get to the middle, you are actually in chapter 22. In other words, all of the topics most associated with Revelation (Antichrist, Armageddon, etc.) are spoken of in the beginning not at the end, which they would be if this project were chronological. I know it sounds a bit confusing, but trust, me this is the best way. The desire is to keep your appetite for the word of God "hot" from the beginning.

What does this book cover? It covers all the basics. The following pages are designed purposefully to be an introduction to the material found in the book of Revelation. Each of the chapters could easily become a book of their own – hey, there's a project for my retirement! All kidding aside, if you find yourself desiring more information regarding a subject matter addressed, feel free to email or call me. I love discussing theological topics, particularly those concerning Revelation.

Enjoy the read and may the "Spirit" be with you . . .

Chapter 1

The Key to the Kingdoms

The Antichrist crushes any and all who do receive his mark. Death and destruction are ever present. The earth and its inhabitants are surviving years of divine judgment. However, one verse from the book of Revelation will change the universe and humanity forever. A cosmic battle of epic proportions commences not with guns, artillery, armies, or demons, but from a trumpet blast. It is a simple statement from a simple angel that declares the future. The only questions is.....Will the remnant persevere?

Although the Book of Revelation, the last book of the Bible, is one of the most easily found books, it is also one of the most difficult books to navigate. Revelation has caused so many questions, but it is also that portion of scripture that gives hope to so many people. Which begs the question: "Why is it that for so many years there has been so much confusion, so much dissension, so much disagreement on what we know as this great book of the Bible, the Book of Revelation?" Many people say it is because Revelation is shrouded in mystery; many people call it the apocalypse. But the Book of Revelation does not start with the apocalypse; it starts with the "revelation" of Jesus Christ. Revelation is not designed by God to hide things from us. In fact, much the opposite is true. Revelation 1:3 says, "Blessed is he that readeath, and they that hear the words of this prophecy, and keep those things which are written therein: for the time is at hand." A blessing is in store for the one who listens to Revelation and then responds in obedience. You see, God's desire is for us to know what is going to happen; God desires for us to receive comfort in the fact that in the end He wins.

So, why is there so much confusion? Believe it or not, the Book of Revelation is the book of the Bible that has more allusions and quotations from the Old Testament than any other book in the New Testament. None of the gospels can compare. In the Book of Revelation (which has 404 verses) there are over 200 references, quotations and allusions to the Old Testament. Most Bible-believing, born again, New Testament Christians will testify that the Old Testament is difficult to read through. When reading through the series of the kings and judges, we fall asleep at the breakfast table. When we see "so-and-so" begat "so-and-so" and begat "so-and-so," we just check out. However, in order to comprehend the contents of Revelation, to gravitate to a truth of understanding, we must be proficient in the Old Testament because the author alludes to it so often throughout the book. Most likely, much of the confusion and chaos in determining the contents of Revelation comes from a lack of Old Testament knowledge.

Yet, we should not allow our lack of knowledge to deter us from further study and examination of scripture. And that is why I have written the book you hold in your hands. Revelation has within its pages a story of intrigue, mystery, hope, loss, death, destruction and redemption. Revelation is the book that reminds us of that once-and-for-all moment when God will make all things new and right. Studying Revelation may not eliminate all of the confusion surrounding the book, but more knowledge and insight will help you gain a greater understanding for the things of God.

> *Revelation is the book that reminds us of that once-and-for-all moment when God will make all things new and right.*

12

Interestingly enough, this particular study of Revelation will not begin in chapter 1 or chapter 2. In fact, this study begins in chapter 11. Why start a study in the middle of the book? Great question!

Do you know that George Lucas, the writer of the *Star Wars* story, began his incredible story in the middle of the saga rather than at the beginning? There are actually six episodes, but the original movie of 1977, that movie that started it all and captured the world's attention with a saga of good versus evil—the dark side and the rebels—started, actually, not with the first episode but with the fourth in hindsight. One of the reasons In my opinion, I believe George Lucas started the *Star*

Wars saga in the middle I believe was because there were certain characters that needed to be fully developed at the mid-point so that viewers could understand how the story would end. And, there were certain characters that would not come on the scene for such a long while, but they still needed to be introduced and developed from the mid-point.

Likewise, Revelation chapter 11 is numerically in the middle of the Book of Revelation, which has twenty-two chapters. Revelation chapter 11, the mid-point of the saga, is critical; for from this point emerges an understanding of the characters and the contents of what is known as the Book of Revelation.

Consider the contents of chapter 11: the Great Tribulation is already underway, a struggle between God's people (marked with the seal of God on their foreheads) and the Antichrist is in play, God's two witnesses arrive on the scene and devour their enemies with fire from their mouths, the witnesses are beheaded and left lying in the street for three and one-half days before being resurrected and raised to heaven. Chapter 11 also describes the contents and size of the new Temple, the city of Jerusalem and the surrounding events. The chapter is packed full of important characters and critical events. Understanding the middle of the story is crucial in comprehending the rest of the saga, from beginning to end.

Chapter 11 is a key chapter. In fact, in Revelation 11:15 something dramatic happens: "And the seventh angel sounded; and there were great voices in heaven, saying, 'The kingdoms of this world are become the kingdoms of our Lord, and of his Christ; and he shall reign for ever and ever.'" Before dealing with the specifics of this

13

simple verse, first understand that in the middle of the Book of Revelation the kingdoms of the world become the kingdom of the Lord. So, in other words, until this point those kingdoms do not belong to the Lord. Understand, as well, that this transfer does not happen at a battle known as Armageddon, nor does it happen at a battle known as Gog and Magog. Hail and fire do not rain from the sky, the sun is not scorched and the moon does not turn dark. In fact, the transfer of the kingdoms takes place along with a consecutive series of divine judgments. For keep in mind that prior to this transfer of kingdoms, the seven seals have been opened, the trumpets of judgment have sounded, and soon the vials, or bowls, will be opened.

However, at this point in the story, between the second and third woes, an angel sounds the seventh trumpet and it is declared that Jesus will reign. It is done. Jesus does not come back and fight at Armageddon so He can have the kingdoms of the world; He has been given the kingdoms of the world and thus Armageddon takes place. Understanding this order of events is an important and critical concept.

In this simple verse, at this declaration in the midst of chaos, the kingdoms of this world have become the kingdoms of our dear Lord. Unpacking Revelation 11:15 will give us an understanding of all the characters, prophecies, and scenarios that are packaged around it within the Book of Revelation. The first thing to consider is the claim to a throne.

CLAIM TO A THRONE
Revelation 11:15 mentions kingdoms being transferred to the Lord Jesus Christ. With kingdoms come the idea and reality of a throne and the one who ultimately claims ownership of that throne. Now,

most reading this live in the United States of America. We are not very familiar with kingdoms and thrones. However, on those rare occasions when someone of royal blood and nature gets married, the whole world watches. Do you realize that in recent days almost one-third of the world, two billion people, watched an elaborate ceremony—the British monarch wedding? Such a wedding is fascinating because it revolves around a kingdom and a throne. Although we, as a country, rebelled against a throne, there is something fascinating about it. When the throne speaks, it happens. From the voice of the throne comes a decree and it is declared throughout the land, there is no voting or negotiating. The throne represents power and rule.

Understand this powerful fact: in the Book of Revelation, some 404 verses, almost ten percent—thirty-nine verses, speak about a throne.

Notice in Revelation 11:15 it says the kingdoms of the world, not the kingdoms of Europe, North America or the kingdoms of those who claim to be believers in Jesus Christ. Understand the impact of this reality. According to Revelation 11:15, there is a throne on which an individual or entity sits who has discretion and rule over all the kingdoms of the world, and at some point these kingdoms are transferred to Jesus Christ. Let this sink in—the throne, which prior to Revelation 11:15 belonged to someone else, is now established in Jesus Christ and He is sitting upon it.

Understand this powerful fact: in the Book of Revelation, some 404 verses, almost ten percent—thirty-nine verses, speak about a throne. One out of every ten verses is alluding to one sitting upon a throne, reigning from a throne, speaking from a throne. This is of huge significance! Of every verse that is found in the Bible that speaks about a throne, twenty-

15

two percent of those verses are found in the Book of Revelation. In other words, one out of every five occurrences to someone sitting on a throne is in Revelation. If all of the passages in Samuel and in Kings about King David and King Solomon and their rules were removed, it would result in almost half of all the passages speaking of a throne being contained within the Book of Revelation. The claim to the throne of the kingdoms of the world is an important theme worth understanding.

Understanding the Past

In order to grasp the significant impact of the "throne" theme, we need to look back, look forward and look at the present. Understand and keep in mind that the Bible is not necessarily written chronologically. In the beginning God did create the heaven and the earth, but understand that by the time Noah and Abraham arrive on the scene, there are other characters who appear—one being a man by the name of Job. The Bible is not necessarily chronological.

Take, for example, a passage of scripture that God gives us from the prophet Isaiah that predates all of what we know as humanity. It predates Adam and Eve and the Garden of Eden. The passage regards the fall of Satan and it is found in Isaiah 14:12-14:

How art thou fallen from heaven, O Lucifer, son of the morning! How are thou cut down to the ground, which didst weaken the nations! For thou has said in thine heart, I will ascend into heaven, I will exalt my throne above the stars of God: I will sit also upon the mount of the congregation, in the sides of the north: I will ascend above the heights of the clouds; I will be like the most High.

The prophecy is given of the future, but Isaiah is also alluding to the past. God can give a prophet insight on the past, not just necessarily foreknowledge of the future. Isaiah 14:13 states that when Satan fell (he was Lucifer before he became Satan) his desire was to establish his throne above God's throne. Now, in the context of Isaiah 14, the prophet Isaiah makes it clear that there was a throne; it was not an imaginary throne. The king of Babylon (and the devil controlling him) literally wanted to place his rule, his authority, his judgment and his verbiage over that which is God's just as Satan wanted to elevate his throne above the Most High's throne. This claim to the throne took place in the past; however, on the other side of the spectrum there is a claim in the future.

The Book of Revelation chapter 21 describes to us that which we long for and sing about—the New Heaven, the New Earth and the New Jerusalem. It speaks about the time when there will be no remembrance of former things. There will be the occasion where there is no more crying, no more weeping, no more heartache, and no more sorrow. You see, Isaiah 14, about the devil himself as he fell, predates what you and I know as humanity in the Garden of Eden. Revelation chapter 21 is on the other side of all the tribulation events. It is on the other side of the Great White Throne Judgment. It is on the other side of the millennium, the other side of the devil, the demons and those who reject Jesus for they have been cast into the bottomless pit, the lake of fire for all eternity. Chapter 21 is on the other side of time as we know it.

Revelation 21:5 says, "And he who sat upon the throne." Chronologically speaking, the Bible has two bookends and they both regard a throne. The Bible has within its contents redemption; it has within its contents salvation. It has within its contents numerous amounts of theological concepts we need to grasp. Understand this, in simplistic terms, the Bible from beginning to end is trying to answer these questions—"Who is in charge and who sits on the throne?"

THE CURRENT SITUATION

The Gospel of Luke chapter 4 describes the forty days and forty nights Jesus spent in the wilderness. At the conclusion of this time, the devil comes and tempts Jesus with various things, one of which is to turn a stone into bread. Another is to throw Himself from the temple peak and to call upon the angels to catch Him so that He does not dash His foot on a rock. In each instance, Satan distorts the context of scripture and tempts Jesus to use His power before the necessarily appointed time. Each time Satan attempts to deter the Lord from God's ultimate plan, Jesus tells the devil to back off and get away from Him. Jesus quotes scripture to refute the temptation.

Notice Luke 4:5, "And the devil, taking him up on a high mountain, showed unto him all the kingdoms of the world." Do you notice a parallel with Revelation 11:15? In Revelation 11:15 the kingdoms of the world are transferred to Jesus Christ. In Luke 4 the devil takes Jesus not to the Mount of Olives so He can see the Middle East, not to Mount Everest where He can see the eastern hemisphere, but to an exceedingly high mountain (we do not know exactly where that may be) and, in a moment of time, Satan shows Christ all the kingdoms of the world.

Luke 4:6 says, "And the devil said unto him, 'All this power I will give thee, and the glory of them: for that is delivered unto me; and to whomsoever I will I give it.'" Clearly, Satan is stating that his throne is upon

18

the kingdoms of the world and he is the ruler, he is in charge and he is reigning. Wait a minute! Doesn't that want to make us step back and say, "No! Don't we sing all these songs about Jesus reigning?" Yes, we do. And, He physically reigns one day, but notice how Jesus responds to the devil: "Get behind me Satan: for it is written, 'Thou shall worship the Lord thy God, and him only shall thou serve.'" Now, understand and keep in mind that Jesus is God in the flesh. Don't you think that if the devil was misquoting something that Jesus could have said, "Devil, you don't know what you are talking about! You don't have any kingdoms; you don't have a throne!" But, Jesus doesn't debate, He doesn't argue, He doesn't put up a fight. Instead, He just says, "Get behind me!"

There is coming a day, and Revelation 11:15 speaks to this, when what the devil tempted Jesus with does come true. Please understand this— the devil was tempting Jesus to do the right thing at the *wrong* time! I want you to gravitate to and understand the fact that if the kingdoms of the world are transferred *to* Jesus Christ that they had to come *from* someone else. But who are these kingdoms transferred from? They are transferred from no less than that person we know as the devil himself!

In John 17, when Jesus is in the Garden of Gethsemane He prays not for the world but for those who will follow in His footsteps. Why? Because before Revelation 21 happens, before that throne is established and all things are made new, Jesus takes possession of this current world and it kingdoms, He abolishes it all in a ball of fire and He remakes a New Heaven, a New Earth and a New Jerusalem. With the simple sound of an angel, when the trumpet sounds in Revelation 11:15, the kingdoms will be given to Jesus.

Now this makes a big difference because when you sit on the throne you possess something that nobody else possesses. You possess a name or a title.

A Title to the Throne

The recent royal wedding incited a world-wide fascination. Close to two million people watched the wedding on some form of internet or television. During the ceremony, roughly 5.4 million internet pages were loading every second because people were searching for details about the wedding. One million people gathered in front of Buckingham Palace to get a glimpse of the wedding party, the groom and the bride. Why are we so fascinated? One commentator summed it up perfectly. When all of the regalia ended, he said, "We now know that for at least the next half-century, the British monarchy is secured." What he was communicating is something that is foreign to us in the United States of America. We do not understand that when there is a king, there is power. The Bible says in Ecclesiastes 8:4, "Where the word of a king is, there is power."

Some years ago, when Prince Charles married Lady Diana, the world was in a frenzy because if something occurs to the Queen of England, Prince Charles is immediately in charge. He would take possession of the throne. Likewise, if something were to occur to the Queen and to Prince Charles, in that order, the man whose marriage recently received world-wide attention would take the throne. Prince William, the Duke of Cambridge is successively the third in line, behind Prince Charles and the present Queen of England, to sit upon the throne. The fascinating story line that captures us is that we know in a heartbeat someone can go from being a prince to a king. In a moment's notice someone's status can change. The American culture does not understand such terminologies in our culture because the lifestyle of a throne does not exist in the United States of America. However, we can understand the fact that kings have the authority to possess the kingdoms of the world; princes do not. Do not forget that before a king is a king—before he takes possession of the throne—he is a prince. Interestingly enough, the prophet Isaiah, roughly eight hundred years before the time of Jesus' birth, life and ministry on earth, wrote that famed verse that we often see on Christmas cards and hear in Christmas songs. Isaiah 9:6 says, "For unto us a child is born, unto us a son is given: and the government shall be upon his shoulder and his name shall be called Wonderful, Counselor, the mighty God, The everlasting Father, The Prince of Peace." Notice, Isaiah does not call Jesus the *King* of Peace. Understand this is why so many people missed Jesus' first coming. As He entered Jerusalem, they hailed Him   21 "King of the Jews," but Isaiah told them He is the *Prince* of Peace.

To understand this concept further, consider what Jesus proclaims in Matthew 10:34 when He says, "Think not that I am come to send peace on earth: I came not to send peace, but a sword." In the midst of discussing His crucifixion and the redemption Jesus would offer us, He proclaims that He did not come to bring peace on the earth in the way that the world would expect it from a king. Instead, the peace Christ offered would come through the redemption that His cross offers us. Romans 5:10 says, "For if, when we were enemies, we were reconciled to God by the death of His Son, much more, being reconciled, we shall be saved by His life." Isaiah proclaimed hundreds and thousands of years ago that Christ would be the Prince of Peace. Jesus testified in His birth, His life and on the cross that peace with God would come through the redemption of sin. The "sword" Jesus brought to the world would eventually lead to peace with God; however, the message of the gospel would bring immediate, earthly conflict—piercing relationships, causing persecution and resulting in martyrdom. However, when Jesus takes physical possession of the kingdoms of the world, He will bring a once-and-for-all peace as the one true, all-powerful King. Revelation 19 alludes to that exciting future moment when Jesus fights as an Almighty King. In that famed battled of Armageddon, Jesus descends out of Heaven. He is gathered on a white horse; He has crowns upon His head. There is a sword pictured coming out of His mouth; His feet are as if brass within judgment. And, most importantly to you and me, the armies of the Lord are behind Him. Now, notice what the Bible says in Revelation 19:16, "And He hath on His vesture and on His thigh a name written, KING OF KINGS, AND LORD OF LORDS." Does the verse say that Jesus is the Prince of Princes? No! It says when He comes He is the King of Kings and Lord of Lords!

What has to happen for a prince to become a king? The throne has to be vacated so it can then be occupied. When the angel sounds in Revelation 11:15 and says the kingdoms have now become, what was taking place is that the current ruler and regulator of all the kingdoms of the world is pushed to the side and Jesus Christ is allowed His presence and His rightful throne. In the past it was prophesied He would be the Prince of Peace; in the future it states He will be the coming King of Kings, and He will be the Lord of Lords. In fact, Revelation 21:24 says, "...and the kings of the earth do bring their glory and honour into it"—*it* being the New Jerusalem. Kings of the earthly kingdoms will come and bow down.

What about our current situation? During the Easter season, we celebrate the sinless life of Jesus and we celebrate His sacrificial death. We celebrate the fact that when any and all call upon His name and say I am a sinner and need a Savior, I am lost and need forgiveness they are saved. We celebrate that truth because He arose from the grave; we can be redeemed; we can be forgiven. We celebrate the fact that He did rise and according to scripture He sits at the right hand of the Father Everlasting to making intercession for us. How do we reconcile these two concepts? He is prophesied to be a Prince of Peace, yet we know that one day He is coming as King of Kings.

Revelation 1:5, one of my favorite verses of scripture, says, "Unto Jesus, who is the faithful witness, and the first begotten of the dead, and the prince of the kings of the earth." Keep in mind, this verse is found at the beginning of the Book of Revelation. The resurrection

> *The only thing we are waiting on is for Jesus to split open the skies and to come back.*

has occurred; the ascension has occurred. The only thing we are waiting on is for Jesus to split open the skies and to come back. And what does the Bible say? The Bible tells us He is the Prince of the kings of the earth—which tells me this: There is coming a day when the angel sounds and at that point all entities, all nations, all rulers, all great and all small will finally once and for all be subject unto His rule, His dominion, His law and His declaration. There is a title which Jesus Christ possesses when this trumpet sounds. When it says the kingdoms of the world have become the kingdoms of our dear Lord, He goes from being the Prince of Peace to the King of Kings; He goes from being the *Prince* of the kings of the earth to the *King* of the kings of the earth. And it happens not because He wins Armageddon; Armageddon is

23

won because it is declared. There is a claim upon a throne throughout the Book of Revelation. There is a declaration of a name or a title.

THE REIGN OF A TERRITORY

That leads us to the final part of the equation: you and me—the reign of a territory. Every king has a kingdom. Revelation 11:15 says "kingdoms of the world," very much in the plural form. In other words, when God speaks of kingdoms of the world He means everything. Don't leave anything out; absolutely all of it is transferred to Christ. The questions we have to ask are these: "What about us? How do we fit into this equation? How do we picture into this kingdom?" It's great to talk about Satan vacating the throne and Jesus reigning. But the territory—the kingdoms of the world—effect you and I as well.

24 Let's take a look into the past. There was a time—the Bible records it in the first couple of chapters of Genesis—that before we sinned, before we rebelled against God, before we said, "God, I think we can do it our way, I think we're smarter than You are, I think we know how to do this thing called life better than You do," there was a day in which the Bible records that humanity, in the person of Adam and Eve, resided in a place called the Garden of Eden. The Bible says they walked there with the Lord in the cool of the day. The Bible says that Adam was given the privilege of naming all of the animals. What you see in that picture is not just a wonderful relationship of God and man walking in the cool of the day, but what you see is the garden and the earth given to them with a king, a ruler; a man by the name of Adam and his bride who would later be name Eve and their children. The anticipation, the desire was for the kingdoms of the world to be theirs. But, we know what happened—sin entered the picture.

The great news about Revelation is this: in the past we sinned; in the past humanity messed up; in the past we gave up the privilege to serve as "kings" of the kingdom, but Jesus Christ redeems us and our position! The story of the cross, the story of the empty tomb is not just limited to our horrific sin and the need to be saved, redeemed and born again. For not only is our sinful condition restored and redeemed but also our status! The Bible declares that because of Jesus Christ, the soon-coming King, the status we voided when we sinned is restored. Revelation 1:5-6 and Revelation 5:10 state that one day you and I, as believers in Jesus Christ, will be in God's kingdom and shall reign with Him. The Bible says in Revelation 19:14-15 that upon Christ's return He will rule the nations of the world with His rod and we shall be in partnership with Him, we shall share the throne with Him. In Revelation 20 the Bible speaks of a thousand years when the devil is locked in the bottomless pit, Jesus sits on His throne in a place known as Jerusalem and the armies of the Lord, you and I, reign with Him. You see, when we rebelled against God in the Garden of Eden, we didn't just guarantee ourselves eternity in a place called hell unless we repented, we also voided the land and the territory He had given to us from the beginning. Sin stripped us of our relationship with God and ripped the territory, the kingdom, away from us as well. The Bible tells us in Romans 8:22 that all of creation groans because of our sin, not just within us but around us. But, when the kingdoms of the world become the kingdoms of our dear Lord, not only does that mean that Jesus is the rightful owner, not only does He sit upon the throne for all eternity, not only does He become the King rather than just the Prince; but that for which we have longed for so many years, that which we voided, that which we allowed to slip out of our fingers shall be returned and redeemed and we shall reign on the earth with Him! We messed up in the past—we know that, but according to the Book of Revelation one day we shall be redeemed—not just spiritually, but in a physical sense as well.

Yet we are still left with our current situation. What about today? There are headlines everywhere; there are signs of the times and all kinds of "end time" scenarios around us—so how do we respond? How do we wake up tomorrow morning and go to the workplace, how do we go to school, how do we go into our homes having all the knowledge of the Antichrist, the millennium, the churches, the concept of a rapture? How does that knowledge change today and tomorrow?

> *We, as the Christian community, are never going to sit on the throne of the kingdoms of the world until He returns.*

26

Simply put, I think it's found in the Book of 2 Corinthians 4:4 which states, "In whom the god of this world hath blinded the minds of them which believe not, lest the light of the glorious gospel of Christ, who is the image of God, should shine unto them." The god of this world, the devil, ravages us on a day by day basis. Understand this: there is a god of this world who sits on the throne of the kingdoms of this world, and his desire is to lead you completely astray from the things of God. He wants to blind you to all the darkness; he wants to blind you to all the truth. He wants to blind you from everything lest the glorious light of Jesus Christ shine in your life.

So how do you respond? Simply put—turn your eyes upon Jesus. How do we respond in the midst of the headlines? Look to Jesus! Titus 2:11-14 states:
> *For the grace of God that bringeth salvation hath appeared to all men, teaching us that, denying ungodliness and worldly lusts,*

we should live soberly, righteously, and godly, in this present world; looking for that blessed hope, and the glorious appearing of the great God and our Saviour Jesus Christ; who gave himself for us, that he might redeem us from all iniquity, and purify unto himself a peculiar people, zealous of good works.

We need to lift our heads up and look to the glorious return of Jesus Christ, because guess what? We, as the Christian community, are never going to sit on the throne of the kingdoms of the world until He returns. We are never going to return with Him until He comes out of the sky so we should not waste our time trying to take over, take in and take out everything, but simply say, "Jesus, work in and through me. May Your light shine and may the darkness be dispelled."

In conclusion, Jesus prayed this in John 17, "Father, I don't pray that You take them out of the world. I just pray that You would keep them from the evil one."

Chapter 2

The Great Tribulation

In the midst of heaven there resides a book sealed with seven seals. Unfortunately, no one on earth or in Heaven is worthy to open its contents. The entire cosmos weeps desiring to know how the great battle will end and what the fate of the universe will be. Then the One who is deemed worthy stands and takes the book and opens the first seal. The four horsemen appear. It is the end of peace. It is the end of prosperity. It is the beginning of the.... Great Tribulation.

The first verse of Revelation begins with these words, "The revelation of Jesus Christ." I believe God wants us, through His Word, to understand the concepts, ideas, characters and battles within Revelation so that we might have hope, peace and comfort in the midst of a life that often does not present a positive picture.

In this chapter we find ourselves in the midst of the book of Revelation. As we study Revelation 6 through 19 we are going to hit some of the highlights and aspects of this section of scripture know as the great tribulation. In order to truly understand it we need to examine other passages of scripture, such as Daniel 9 and Matthew 24-25.

In Matthew 24 and 25, we find ourselves at the end of Jesus' earthly ministry. In fact, we are just a couple of days from the crucifixion; we are just a couple of days from Judas' betrayal of Jesus and the cruel reality of Christ upon the cross. Jesus gathers His disciples, that inner group that had been with Him for over three years, on the Mount of Olives, literally a stone's throw away from the eastern gate of the Temple Mount. As they looked down at that Temple and all of the festivities of the Passover week, the disciples ask Jesus a set of very important questions such as what will be the sign of Your return, and what will be the end of the world as we know it?

Jesus' response is familiar to us even if we have not studied the Book of Revelation and "the end times." He describes the idea that there will be wars and rumors of wars, there will be earthquakes in diverse places, the sun will change color as well as the moon, the stars will fall out of the sky, and children will not only disrespect but literally turn on their parents. He describes a time of chaos; He describes a time of horrific events on earth. In Matthew 24:15 Jesus makes this statement: "And when you see the abomination of desolation spoken of by the prophet Daniel..." In the midst of all the teachings of the second coming, all the teachings of prophecy, Jesus alludes back to the prophet Daniel. Then He begins to elaborate: flee, run, take to the hills! In other words, it's going to be bad. In Matthew 24:21 Jesus says, "For then shall be great tribulation, such as was not since the beginning of the world to this time, no, nor ever shall be." When the great tribulation occurs it is worse than anything that has ever happened or will ever happen.

> *When the great tribulation occurs it is worse than anything that has ever happened or will ever happen.*

32

Keep in mind that Jesus calls this the great tribulation.

So, when we study Revelation, chapters 6 through 19, when we study this event that contains the famous seven seals and trumpets and such, understand that it was not a theologian that gave this time period its name; it was not a church, a denomination or a pastor. It was Jesus Christ Himself who described this event, as prophesied in Daniel and fulfilled in Revelation, as the great tribulation.

AN EXPLANATION OF THE GREAT TRIBULATION

In Daniel chapter 9, beginning in verse 24 we read about the seventy weeks—the seventy weeks refers to a time period. Most commentators agree that Daniel's prophesy is speaking of years of chronology. The total time period, seventy times seven, is four hundred ninety years in length. It is divided in several sections. Daniel is speaking prophetically of years in the future. Daniel 9:24-27 states:

Seventy weeks are determined upon thy people and upon thy holy city, to finish the transgression, and to make an end of sins, and to make reconciliation for iniquity, and to bring in everlasting righteousness, and to seal up the vision and prophecy, and to anoint the most Holy. Know therefore and understand, that from the going forth of the commandment to restore and to build Jerusalem unto the Messiah the Prince shall be seven weeks, and threescore and two weeks: the street shall be built again, and the wall, even in troublous times. And after threescore and two weeks shall Messiah be cut off, but not for himself: and the people of the prince that shall come shall destroy the city and the sanctuary; and the end thereof shall be with a flood, and unto the end of the war desolations are determined. And he shall confirm the covenant with many for one week: and in the midst of the week he shall cause the sacrifice and the oblation to cease, and for the overspreading of abominations he shall make it desolate, even until the consummation, and that determined shall be poured upon the desolate.

33

Itinerary of the Great Tribulation

When Jesus spoke in Matthew 24 about the abomination of desolation, He is speaking specifically of the prophecy in Daniel 9:27. Any time you are going to experience a trip, an endeavor, or a journey you need to set an itinerary so that you know what to expect at a particular time. In the midst of the prophecy of Daniel, it says that in this final week, in the midst of the week, that he, the Antichrist or the beast that comes out of the bottomless pit, makes a covenant that is broken and commits the abomination of desolations.

The great tribulation is a time period that is seven years in length. Based on Daniel 9:27, the first three and one-half years of the tribulation, for a lack of a better term, are "not that bad." But, the second three and one-half years when the abomination of desolation takes place, Jesus says in Matthew 24:16 to run to the hills! In other words, "Get out of here because it has never been nor will it ever be this bad again!"

There comes a point in the midst of the great tribulation (in the midst of this Antichrist figure convincing the world that he is worthy to be followed and to welcomingly receive his mark so that they can have trade and commerce) when there is a drastic turn of events. There is a point in which the Antichrist reveals his true identity and he shows himself for what he really is. According to the itinerary in Daniel 9:27, that change happens in the middle of this week. Understand that in the midst of the seven year great tribulation the first three and one-half years are not that bad, per se, but the last three and one-half are literally horrific.

Intent of the Great Tribulation

Daniel 9:24 says to finish the transgression, to make an end of sins, to make reconciliation for iniquity, to bring in everlasting righteousness, to seal up the vision and the prophecy, and to anoint the most Holy. Without going into graphic detail on every one of those phrases or points, I believe that the purpose of this time period is to eradicate not only sin but the one who is the author of sin, Satan, and to establish the most High, the King of kings and the Lord of lords, Jesus Christ. The purpose of the great tribulation is to rid the world, once and for all, of sin and then to usher in the reign of Jesus Christ.

I think the question that could be the most valuable for us to answer is this: Who are the individuals who will endure this horrific event for seven years? For whom is the great tribulation intended?

Daniel 9:24 says that seventy weeks are determined "upon thy people." Second Timothy 2:15 says that we are to rightly divide the Word of God. When the Bible speaks of thy people or the people of God, it is calling or describing those people who were called out in Genesis 12 and 15; Abraham, Isaac, Jacob, the twelve tribes, what we know as the chosen people, the people of God, the Israelites, the Jewish community. There is a distinction between the *people* of God and the children of God. John 1:12 says those who believe on Jesus would be called the *children of God.* Keep in mind that John 1:11 says that Jesus came to His own, but His own did not receive Him. There is a distinction between being *the people of God* and being *the children of God.*

> *The purpose of the great tribulation is to rid the world, once and for all, of sin and then to usher in the reign of Jesus Christ.*

35

Now the reason I address the distinction between the people of God and the children of God is that in the book of Daniel, in the book of Matthew, chapter 24 and, in particular, in Revelation, chapters 6 through 19, there is not one reference to the church of Jesus Christ.

There is not one reference to the *children* of God suffering the wrath of God, but there is reference to the *people* of God who have rejected the Messiah, Jesus Christ, enduring this horrific time period.

Initiation of the Great Tribulation

The great tribulation is the seven year itinerary with the intent of pushing out sin and ushering in the King of kings and the Lord of lords upon those individuals who have for millennia rejected the Messiah, Jesus Christ. How does the time period of the great tribulation start? After all, Daniel 9 says there is a gap of time between the Messiah being cut off and this final week. What initiates the final week?

36 Chapters 4 and 5 of the Book of Revelation are different than all of the other chapters. All of the other chapters take place on earth; they take place with the events occurring on the "dirt." But in Revelation chapters 4 and 5 we are in the throne room. We see the throne of God, the thunders, the lightening, all the things that make heaven an incredible place—the crystal sea, the cherubim singing, the angels singing, the martyrs singing. It is a fabulous worship experience!

In Revelation chapter 5 a book is presented; the book with those famous seven seals. A loud angel proclaims in Heaven, in earth and below the earth, "Who is worthy to open the book?" No one was found worthy. The Apostle John begins to weep because this book with seven seals has the answers to the end of the world, the conclusion of the great cosmic battle between God and Satan and those who choose their respective sides. Then, there was One that stood; there was One that was slain as a Lamb from the tribe of Judah. The person who takes the book in Revelation chapter 5 is Jesus Christ, the Lamb that was slain.

That leads us to Revelation 6:1, the beginning of the tribulation, the initiation: "When the Lamb opened one of the seals, and I heard, as it were the noise of thunder, one of the four beasts saying, Come and see." Now this is very relevant for us because the *same* Jesus who lived for us, the *same* Jesus who went to the cross for us, the *same* Jesus who quoted John 3:16, said, "I will never leave you, I will never forsake you, my yoke is easy and my burden is light." The *same* Jesus who calls us His children, the *same* Jesus who healed the sick and walked on water and said, "Suffer the little children to come unto me," the *same* Jesus who gave women rights when the society did not, the *same* Jesus who gave those on the bottom of the socioeconomic scale the ability to listen to the same things that those on the upper-crust heard is the *same* One who opens the seals!

This picture of Jesus is much different than His earthly ministry. This is not a Jesus coming to demonstrate His great love for mankind; this is a Jesus coming to open the seals and pour out the wrath of God on those who have rejected Him. The picture that we have in Revelation 6 is that the initiation, the beginning of what we know as the great tribulation, does not occur because the Antichrist shows up; the Antichrist shows up because Jesus opens the seals. The great tribulation does not occur because we have reached that chronological time on the calendar; it is that chronological time on the calendar because Jesus stands up and opens the seals. Understand this—the great tribulation starts with Jesus Christ; He initiates it.

37

Escalation of the Great Tribulation

Jesus initiates the great tribulation, and then there is an escalation of the events. In chapter 6 and chapter 7 we have the famous seven seals being opened. In fact, there are three major series of judgments in chapters 6 through 19; there are the seven seals, the seven trumpets, and the seven bowls or vials. There are two major opinions on this subject matter. One of those opinions is that as you read through the seals, as you read through the trumpets and as you read through the vials that the story of the tribulation is told three consecutive times. In other words, when the seals are opened, it is the surface level. When the trumpets are opened, it is the mid-range. But the vials, in Revelation chapter 16, are really the nitty-gritty of how bad this time period will be.

That is one theory. Personally speaking, I believe in what I call the escalation theory. I believe that the seals open up the trumpets and the trumpets open up the vials. What I mean by that is actually found in Revelation chapter 8.

When that seventh seal is opened, the angelic beings, these cherubim who were constantly praising God saying, "Holy, Holy, Holy, Lord God Almighty, who is, who was and who is to come," suddenly become silent. Revelation 8:2 says, "And I saw the seven angels which stood before God; and to them were given seven trumpets." Revelation chapters 8, 9 and 11 describe the trumpet judgments and later in chapter 16 the vials are introduced. I am of the opinion that during this seven week itinerary there is an escalation of events as we go from day to day, week to week and year to year.

Things do not just mellow out, they do not just plateau, they actually get worse.

Devastation of the Great Tribulation

Revelation chapter 16 describes the devastation of the great tribulation. No matter which theory you subscribe to—whether you believe the tribulation is told three different ways or if you believe in the escalation of events—when the vials are introduced, this is as bad as it gets. At the end of the escalation is the devastation.

The first vial is opened in Revelation 16:2. "And the first went, and poured out his vial upon the earth; and there fell a noisome and grievous sore upon the men which had the mark of the beast, and upon them which worshipped his image." Now I don't know about you but 39 when I read that, it does not sound like fun. There comes a point when the first vial is opened and the mark of the beast will be "opened up and there is a noisome and grievous sore." That is a devastation event.

Revelation 16:3 says, "And the second angel poured out his vial upon the sea; and it became as the blood of a dead man: and every living soul died in the sea." This is not just an environmental hazard; this is not just a mistake by industry that affects us. The Bible says every living soul in the sea died. This is a completely devastating event. Revelation 16:4 says, "And the third angel poured out his vial upon the rivers and fountains of waters; and they became blood." Revelation 16:8 says, "And the fourth angel poured out his vial upon the sun; and power was given unto him to scorch men with fire." I don't know how you want to coat it, couch it or claim it—this is a devastating time period. The end of the seven year period, known as the great tribulation, is a horrific and devastating time for any and all. There are sores upon the head, water is turned into blood (you cannot eat anything found in water), and the sun is scorching. Keep in mind that at this point only four out of the seven vials have been opened. It is a truly devastating event.

Protection of the Great Tribulation

Jesus initiates it, it escalates and it is devastating. But the next point I want to address is critical: in the midst of all of this there is also the protection of the great tribulation. Even in the Old Testament in the Book of Exodus when those plagues were poured out on the Egyptian people, God told the Israelites to go to the land of Goshen. If they went to Goshen they would not be harmed. Revelation 14:1 says, "And I looked, and lo, a Lamb stood on the mount Sion (Jesus), and with him an hundred forty and four thousand (that famous number), having his Father's name written in their foreheads."

Now let me draw a distinction here. In the midst of the tribulation those who would turn to God are protected; those who would reject the mark of the beast are protected. But notice how they are protected: the name of the Father is in their forehead. If you are right now, or you are soon to become a born-again Christian, you have admitted that you have sinned, you know you have strayed from God, and you have asked Jesus to save you. Understand this: nowhere in the Bible; not in Romans, Galatians, Ephesians, Philippians, Colossians, etc. — nowhere in the New Testament is there any evidence that a born-again Christian ever gets the name of the Father in his forehead. In fact, the

Bible says that our body is the temple of God who resides within us, and we are a new creation in Him.

The reason I draw that distinction is that the Bible does not describe those who are protected during the tribulation in the same way that you and I presently are described. The Bible does say that even in the midst of the horrific time period of seven years that those few souls (144,000) who say they are not going the way of the Antichrist and they will not take his mark even if it hurts them, will have the seal of God in their forehead. Even in the midst of tribulation God protects them.

Conclusion of the Great Tribulation

> *Jesus initiates it*
> *and Jesus*
> *concludes it.*

Jesus initiates the great tribulation, it escalates, there is devastation, there is 41 protection, but there is also a conclusion of the great tribulation. Jesus initiates it and Jesus concludes it. The tribulation ends in Revelation 19:11 when the Bible says that the heavens split and Jesus comes pictured as riding on a horse with a sword out of His mouth, with His feet as brass, His armies (very key) behind Him, establishing what we know as the Battle of Armageddon and eventually His reign. That seven year time period starts with Jesus opening the first seal and He ends it when He comes back at His second coming.

I often heard my mother say, "I brought you into the world and I will take you out." You may have heard similar words! That is why so many people are truly fearful of mama! I have seen six feet-five, three hundred pound football players cry in front of their four-feet-eleven mamas. Why? It doesn't matter what her size is, they know "mama can just take you out."

Here in the tribulation it is important to know Jesus started it and Jesus finishes it. The tribulation does not end when "the devil gets tired." It does not end when "the calendar strikes a certain day." It does not end because people get exhausted or there is so much havoc. It ends when Jesus says it ends and it is finished. The great tribulation is started by Him and it is ended by Him.

A TIME OF REJECTION

The great tribulation is also a time of rejection. Revelation 16:9 and 11 say, "And men were scorched with great heat, and blasphemed the name of God, which has power over these plagues: and they repented not to give him glory… And blasphemed the God of heaven because of their pains and their sores, and repented not of their deeds."

Every one of us at some level and at some point in life (whether it is a completely objective third-party or someone whom we intimately know) has seen someone make bad decisions and poor choices—continuing to place themselves in a position where they are just "sliding down the hill" and going the wrong way quickly. How many times, whether we actually know them or not, have we made this statement to ourselves: "When are they going to wake up, when are they finally going to real-ize how bad it's getting, when are they going to stop the madness?"

You know, we can say the same thing about the great tribulation. How many seals does it really take in order for God to get your attention? How many trumpets have to sound before you realize you are headed the wrong way? How many vials have to be poured out for you to say: "This is not working for me. This whole loyalty to the Antichrist thing is going the wrong way. Those who worship the One who is pouring out the plagues are okay and I am not."

How many times would we look at this situation and say, "What is wrong with these people, why didn't they pay attention? They still blaspheme God; they still refuse to repent of their sins."

The great tribulation is that time period that will occur at some point in the near future. But I think we can still learn a lesson from its message: at different levels and in different positions God is trying to get our attention. We get upset about life and some of the pains and struggles of life and sometimes we just dismiss it. Maybe in the quietness of your life you

> *The unrepentant in Revelation still blasphemed God; they still did not repent of their sins.*

have said it's not bad enough yet. Have you become the proverbial frog in the kettle? If you take a pot of boiling water and throw a frog in it, he's going to jump right out. But if you take a pot of lukewarm, room-temperature water, put a frog in it and slowly turn up the heat then that frog gets so acclimated to its environment that it literally boils to death because it doesn't realize what's happening to it.

Maybe today you are one of those who has said I know what I need to do with God, I know I need to repent, I know I need Jesus in my life, I know I need to get serious about the things of God but if it gets any worse, then I'll do it. It will get worse. And it will continue to get worse. And the problem is you are literally boiling and you don't

43

even realize it. Let me encourage you today: don't fall into the trap of saying surely it won't get any worse because as it gets worse and worse, it gets harder and harder to turn to God. The unrepentant in Revelation still blasphemed God; they still did not repent of their sins. Would this be that day when you say enough is enough? Would this be the day when you say, "God, I'm done; I'm done rebelling against You; I'm done being contrary to You; I'm done swimming in sin; I'm done saying no to You."

Would this be the day when you say, "Okay, I'm repenting; I will no longer blaspheme. You are not going to have to turn up the heat anymore—today I turn to You." Learn a lesson from those in the future and apply it to your life today.

44

Chapter 3

The Antichrist

In the midst of the Great Tribulation one appears who provides answers to the universe's problems. Miracles, wonders, and signs verify his promises. The rulers of the world are enamored with him. The majority of humanity identifies themselves with him. All of life for a brief time revolves around him. There is a mark. There is a number. Most importantly there is a deception. How long will it be before the universe discovers they have been betrayed not by a hero but by . . . the Antichrist.

Revelation 13 is a study of one of the most famous characters in the world. One day this character will arise in great power. Initially he will bring peace, but that peace is a counterfeit peace. Shortly after his rise to power, his reputation will change. He will be known as the man who deceives, who is depraved, who instills a mark and a number on his followers, and who destroys all who reject him. This person is known best as the Antichrist—a mystifying character that appears on the scene during the great tribulation time. Many people attempt to postulate or presume the actual identity or person of the Antichrist. Some have attempted to declare a specific date when the Antichrist will rise to power. You will find none of that throughout the pages of this book. Instead, we will dive into the scripture to determine what the Bible has to say about this famed character. In fact, in Revelation 13, beginning with verse 11, we find in context an entire chapter dedicated to this person, the Antichrist. Revelation 13:11-18 reads:

47

> And I beheld another beast coming up out of the earth; and he had two horns like a lamb, and he spoke as a dragon. And he exercised all the power of the first beast before him, and caused the earth and them which dwell therein to worship the first beast, whose deadly wound was healed. And he doeth great wonders, so that he made fire come down from heaven on the earth in the sight of men, And deceived them that dwell on the earth, that they should make an image to the beast, which had the wound by a sword, and did live. And he had power to give life unto the image of the beast, that the image of the beast should both speak, and cause that as many as would not worship the image of the beast should be killed.

And he causes all, both small and great, rich and poor, free and bond, to receive a mark in their right hand, or in their forehead: And that no man might buy or sell, save he that had the mark, or the name of the beast, or the number of his name. Here is wisdom. Let him that hath understanding count the number of the beast: for it is the number of a man; and his number is Six hundred threescore and six.

WHO IS THE ANTICHRIST?

Revelation 13 is a famed chapter of scripture about an individual known collectively as the Antichrist. There have been books written in numerous volumes that describe intricate details about this character. Such books also state comparisons and postulate about the identity of this particular person. There is great discussion and debate in our society about the Antichrist and his rise to power.

> *The Antichrist is a person not merely an organization or institution.*

48

Comparing, postulating and debating can often overwhelm us and complicate an issue. Therefore, I would like to present a more simplistic approach to this very complex subject matter by addressing two very simple questions in hopes to provide clarity and a better understanding of this mysterious character known as the Antichrist. The first question is simply, "Who is the Antichrist?" And second, "What is this famous mark of the beast?"

The Antichrist is a Person

The first thing to grasp about the Antichrist is this—the Antichrist is a person who will one day arrive on the scene. Notice what is said in

Revelation 13:18,"...for it is the number of a man." There are many who say the Antichrist is really just a terminology for an institution or the terminology for an organization. Now, let me give credence: Revelation 13 and the Book of Daniel chapter 7, both prophesy that the Antichrist will woo the world. He will have a legion of kings behind him. He will have the nations in support of him, and the institutions and organizations of the world will be at his beck and call--he will have them in his back pocket. However, know this: the Antichrist is a person not merely an organization or institution. The Bible says in Revelation 13:18 that he is an individual who has a name and a number.

The name "Antichrist" is not found anywhere in the Book of Revelation. In fact, there are only a few places in the Bible where the term "Antichrist" exists. 1 John 2:18-19 says:

> *Little children, it is the last time: and as ye have heard that*   49
> *Antichrist shall come, even now are there many Antichrists;*
> *whereby we know that it is the last time. They went out from*
> *us, but they were not of us: for if they had been of us, they*
> *would no doubt have continued with us: but they went out,*
> *that they might be made manifest that they were not all of us.*

Notice the first occurrence of the term "Antichrist" refers to that one individual who will rule the world in the final days. The passage also refers to those last days when there will be people who claim to have once had the faith but left it; they were never a part of the faith and they are Antichrists trying to distort the truth of Christ. The Bible says in 2 John 7, "For many deceivers are entered into the world, who confess not that Jesus Christ is come in the flesh. This is a deceiver and an Antichrist." Those who deny that Jesus Christ came in the flesh are against Christ, anti-Christ, and thus an Antichrist. In 2 Thessalonians, the Bible describes this person known as the Antichrist as the son of perdition, the man of sin, the man of lawlessness. However, in the Book of Revelation the Antichrist is not called the son of perdition, he is not called the man of lawlessness, and he is not called the man of sin. In fact, he is not even called the Antichrist. Instead, he is called the beast. Why is it that God would take that name, that adjective, and describe him as the beast? I believe the Book of Daniel holds the answer. You see, the prophecies in Daniel of the Antichrist figure refer to him as that final beast that will rise up out of the sea and deceive the masses. In the Book of Revelation, the Antichrist is a person with a name; that name is "beast." The term "Antichrist" is not in the Book of Revelation; however, "Antichrist" is a term that is used collectively to describe this character. I think we have free license to use the term "Antichrist" when describing this character named the beast in Revelation. The "beast" as seen in Revelation is against Christ. In other words, he is anti-Christ and *anti* all that is associated with Christ. Thus, the beast described in Revelation is the Antichrist.

The Antichrist has a Number

Revelation tells us the Antichrist has a name, the beast, but he also has a number: 666. Most people, whether they attend church or not, are familiar with that famous number. Interestingly enough, many people have attempted to prove the identity of the Antichrist using the number 666. You see, many languages place numerical values on the letters within the alphabet. Hebrew, Greek and Latin are three such languages. For example, in Latin the letter "I" has the value of 1, the letter "X" has the value of 10, the letter "V" has the value of 5, and the letter "M" has the value of 1,000. Each Latin letter has an assigned numerical value. Likewise, Hebrew and Greek letters have numerical values; however, English letters do not have assigned numerical values. That being said, finding a person's name with the numeric value of 666 is not very difficult. In fact, throughout history there have been characters with names that carry the numeric value of 666.

For example, Nero, a character from the first century, has a name with the numeric value of 666. Does this make him the Antichrist? There is one problem with that theory—Nero died in A.D. 68 and John was on the island of Patmos in A.D. 96. You see, when God gave John the visions written within the Book of Revelation Nero was already dead and gone. Yet, there were other rulers that came after Nero. Could they have been the Antichrist? Six to seven hundred years after Nero, there was a man who took the world by storm in a religious fashion. 51 He is known as Muhammad, the founder of the Islamic religion. If you take Muhammad's full name and translate the letters from English to Latin letters, assign the numeric values of those particular letters and add those values together the sum total equals 666! To take this a step further, about 1,000 years later, a man by the name Martin Luther and some of the legends of the faith began to take the Bible and translate it into the common languages of the day—German and English. These men made an interesting discovery concerning the Latin message written on the hat of the Pope in the Vatican. By removing the vowel letters from the message and adding up the numeric values of the remaining consonants, the sum total equals 666! But it does not stop there. Believe it or not, the name Ronald Wilson Reagan also has the numeric value of 666! Finding the numeric value of 666 in any name is fairly easy to manipulate. Simply find a language that has numeric values, match that value to a person's name, and there you have it—666! It seems like any high profile character today that has any amount of Biblical Christianity against him is labeled Antichrist, and somehow the numeric value of his name totals 666.

So, what is this famous number? Can we really understand what it means? After all, it does say in Revelation chapter 13 that "six hundred threescore and six," 666, is the number of the Antichrist; it is the mark of the beast. Keep in mind that within the Book of Revelation there are over 200 quotations, illustrations or allusions that refer back to the Old Testament. Every illustration within Revelation is an Old Testament illustration. Amazing! In fact, those Jewish individuals alive during the time of the great tribulation (those who are part of that famous 144,000 from the twelve tribes of Israel) should understand the allusions because they come from that with which they are familiar—the Old Testament.

Keep in mind that other than Solomon declaring that he had 666 talents of gold in his bank chest, there is only one other passage of scripture in the Bible that has the number 666. Why is this significant? I believe we can fall into error when we begin to interpret the Bible by going outside of the Bible rather than letting the Bible give us our answers. Therefore, looking into the Bible for clarification on the number 666 leads us to the Book of Ezra. Now keep in mind that in the Book of Ezra the Israelite people are coming out of captivity (Nebuchadnezzar and the Babylonians took them into captivity). Ezekiel and Daniel were two prophets there as well. The Persian king, Cyrus, allows the Israelites to go back home, and Nehemiah rebuilds the wall. The prophet Ezra reestablishes the priesthood and the scriptures. Ezra chapter 2 lists everyone who came back to Jerusalem. Each family name is listed with the number of family members who returned home. Ezra 2:13 says, "The children of Adonikam, six hundred sixty and six."

One of the things that our culture has lost to a degree, and my family is guilty of it, is that we have lost giving names to our children based on the name and its meaning. Instead, names are given because it is a family member's name. Names are given because we want to remember someone who was dear to us. Surprisingly enough, my legal name Jeffrey means "the gift of peace." (By the way, my wife and mother are the only people who are allowed to call me Jeffrey! My name is Jeff!) For those that know me, my somewhat high-strung personality does not really typify what we think of as "peace and quiet." Consider this: my wife's name is Traci. Traci means "brave one." You have to be the brave one to be married to me, I will testify to that! My oldest son's name, Marshall, means "keeper of horses." Why did we name him Marshall? Because that was his grandmother's maiden name, and we wanted to remember a name that had been lost.

> *This person who will deceive the world and force everyone to take his mark if they want to buy or sell anything—this is the lord of rebellion.*

However, in most cultures, particularly in the eastern world, names have a significant meaning. That brings me back to the name Adonikam mentioned in Ezra 2:13. Are you ready for this? The name Adonikam means "lord of rebellion." The only other place where the famed 666 is used in scripture in reference to humanity is when it talks about a person who is the lord of rebellion.

53

In a study of the Antichrist as seen in Revelation 13, we are not admonished or encouraged to identify a particular person in history and to claim that he is the Antichrist. Instead, we need to understand that this character who will perform miracles, wonders and signs; this person who will deceive the world and force everyone to take his mark if they want to buy or sell anything—this is the lord of rebellion. The problem we fall into is this: every time we put a popular name with that famed number 666 we discredit ourselves, our testimony and the testimony of prophecy. Simply stated, the Antichrist has a name; he is the beast. He has a number; it is 666.

The Antichrist has a Philosophy

A study of the Antichrist does not just stop with the fact that he has a name and number. It goes beyond his person; the Antichrist also has a philosophy. He is an imitator. After all, he is Satan incarnate; he is the devil incarnate. Revelation 6 describes the opening of the first of the seven seals. There are seven seals, seven trumpets and seven vials, or bowls, opened. When Jesus Christ, the only One who is found worthy to open the book with the seven seals, opens the first seal what comes out is the person we know as the Antichrist, the beast—he is the first beast that comes after the seal is opened. Revelation 6:1-2 says, "And I saw when the Lamb opened one of the seals, and I heard, as it were the noise of thunder, one of the four beasts saying, 'Come and see.' And I saw, and behold a white horse: and he that sat on him had a bow; and a crown was given unto him: and he went forth conquering, and to conquer."

Notice the unparalleled imitation. The famous Battle of Armageddon is initiated when Jesus Christ splits the eastern sky and He comes out of the clouds. How does He come? On a donkey? No, that was Palm Sunday. On a mule? No. Well, then how does He come? He comes on a white horse. In Revelation 6 the Antichrist is pictured on a white horse. He has a crown upon his head. Revelation 19 describes Jesus Christ with many crowns upon His head. The beast is also followed by death and famine. However, Jesus Christ is followed by the armies of heaven. What we know about the Antichrist, the beast from the Book of Revelation, is that he does not come with a red suit, horns and a tail. He comes imitating the real King; he comes imitating the real Lord. He is nothing but an imitator. He personifies himself as the answer when he is the false identity.

Not only does the Antichrist imitate, but his imitation leads to an illusion; he acts almost as a magician. Revelation 13:13 says, "And he doeth great wonders, so that he maketh fire come down from heaven on the earth in the sight of men." Does that sound familiar? The prophet Elijah, through the power of God, also brought fire from heaven. Keep in mind, the devil has never had an original thought; he only knows how to imitate the real deal. Revelation 13:14 tells us that the Antichrist deceives those that dwell on the earth through signs and wonders. Second Thessalonians chapter 2 reminds us that the man of sin, the son of perdition, the Antichrist performs amazing signs and wonders that cause the world to follow him.

Allow me to share with you my belief about the Antichrist. He will be what the world—those who refuse to believe in Jesus Christ and the Bible—will claim as their messiah. He will be the one with the answers

55

to all their problems. He will be the one with the solutions to all their struggles. He will be the one who can cure, heal and do miracles; he will pull together what has been torn apart. He comes with signs; he comes with wonders. Guess what? Those who rejected Jesus Christ because He came in humility (which was quite different from the way they expected a Messiah to arrive on the earthly scene) will embrace the Antichrist because he will fulfill their expectations of a king.

Recall the account when Jesus was on the side of the mountain and those around Him wanted a sign; just one more sign (as if walking on water and feeding five thousand wasn't enough!). They wanted more. Jesus said, "I'll show you one and only one sign. As Jonah was in the belly of the whale for three days and three nights, I'll be in the heart of the earth three days and three nights." When Jesus rose from the dead, He easily could have said, "You want a sign? There's your sign."

A complete reading of Revelation 13 will show you that the beast receives a deadly wound and comes back to life. Once again there is an imitation and illusion. The Antichrist uses a deceitful trick in which he dupes humanity, both the "wise and intelligent," the small and the tall, the grand and those who are enslaved; everyone falls for his ruse. Let me ask again, "Who is the Antichrist?" He is the one who will come one day; the world will think he is the Messiah, but he is nothing more than the deceiver.

WHAT IS THE MARK OF THE BEAST?

Notice that the term used in the Book of Revelation is the "mark of the beast" not the mark of the Antichrist. Revelation 13:16-18 says:

And he causes all, both small and great, rich and poor, free and bond, to receive a mark in their right hand, or in their foreheads. And that no man might buy or sell, save he that had the mark, or the name of the beast, or the number of his name. Here is wisdom. Let him that has understanding count the number of the beast: for it is the number of a man; and his number is six hundred sixty-six.

Placement of the Mark of the Beast

I want to address something you may have never noticed while reading or studying your Bible: it is the placement of this famous mark of the beast. Understand, Revelation 13:16 is translated in one of two ways: the verse either reads "in" the forehead or right hand or "on" the 57 forehead or right hand. Interestingly enough, the King James Version of the Bible is the only version that uses the word "in." Why is that significant? Recently we celebrated the four hundredth anniversary of what we know as the greatest piece of English literature that man ever gave us—what we know as the King James Version of the Bible. Obviously the word "on" is different than the word "in." So, why is the word "in" used in the King James Version of the Bible? Allow me, if you will, to give an explanation by providing a brief lesson in Biblical languages. The Greek word *epi* used in Revelation 13:16 is translated "in." *Epi* is a simple preposition used over 600 times in the New Testament. However, *epi* does not have a definitive definition. *Epi* means "in, on, under, through and within." *Epi* also means "through this, over that, and under this." You see, *epi* can only be defined within the context of how it is used.

For example, in Philemon 1:4 the Apostle Paul makes this statement, "I remember you always *epi* my prayers." Paul probably did not mean that he remembers people "under" his prayers or "over" his prayers. No, he probably meant that he remembers people "in" his prayers. Furthermore, when Jesus preaches His first sermon in Luke 4 and quotes the Old Testament Book of Isaiah He says, "The spirit of the Lord is *epi* Me;" is "upon" Me. The only way that you can translate the word epi with accuracy is to translate the word in context.

So, in 1611 when those brilliant men gave us what we know as the King James Version of the Bible, they used the word "in" when they translated Revelation 13:16. Keep in mind the hypodermic needle was 200 years from being invented; before that there was no physical way to actually put something in the body's skin or veins. In the late 1800s and early 1900s when the forefathers translated all of the other new versions of the English bible, they translated the word *epi* to "on" because at that particular time in history we did not have the ability to put things in the body. However, here is an interesting fact: some people own pets with microchips inside of their bodies. Today, presently, we have hypodermic needles. Most likely diabetic individuals are very thankful for the hypodermic needle and insulin. Insulin can now be placed into the body and save lives!

Why am I chasing this rabbit? Because I believe the person of the Antichrist will be the most subtle, most stealthy, most deceptive person who has ever walked the planet. Four hundred years ago when those brilliant men sat down to translate the King James Version of the Bible, they were faced with this word *epi*. I imagine they wondered something like, "Does it mean on, under, through or in?" Maybe they thought

58

this: "Even if we don't understand how the beast can do this—place a mark in the body—he is crafty. If he does miracles and wonders and if he feigns coming back from the dead, then somehow he can figure out this particular situation." You see, the placement of the famed mark of the beast is going to be so deceptive that I do not believe anyone will be able to walk around in those days and determine who has the mark and who does not. Jesus told an interesting story about wheat and tares, or weeds. Matthew 13:24-30 says this:

> *Another parable put he forth unto them, saying, "The kingdom of heaven is likened unto a man which sowed good seed in his field: But while men slept, his enemy came and sowed tares among the wheat, and went his way. But when the blade was sprung up, and brought forth fruit, then appeared the tares also. So the servants of the householder came and said unto him, 'Sir, didst not thou sow good seed in thy field? From whence then hath it tares?' He said unto them, 'An enemy hath done this.' The servants said unto him, 'Wilt thou then that we go and gather them up?' But he said, 'Nay; lest while ye gather up the tares, ye root up also the wheat with them. Let both grow together until the harvest: and in the time of harvest I will say to the reapers, 'Gather ye together first the tares, and bind them in bundles to burn them: but gather the wheat into my barn.'"*

59

You see, wheat and tares, or a type of weed, look the same on the outside. In fact, in the story that Jesus tells, the wheat and tares grow up beside one another and no one can tell them apart until the harvest; however, one day the sickle is going to come and judgment is going to happen.

On that day a true distinction will be made between the "wheat" and the "tares."

Revelation 14:1 says, "And I looked, and, lo, a Lamb stood on the mount Sion, and with him an hundred forty and four thousand, having his Father's name written in their foreheads." Understand this fact: those who reject the mark of the beast will have the name of the Father in their foreheads instead of the mark of the beast. If someone in the days of the great tribulation is walking around with the number 666 plastered on his head, it would be easy to determine that he is associated with the Antichrist, the evil one. I believe making a distinction between who is "wheat" and who are "tares" during the great tribulation will be difficult if that decision is based merely on physical, outward appearance. Allow me to state it once again, the placement of the famed mark of the beast is going to be so deceptive that I do not believe anyone will be able to walk around in those days and determine who has the mark and who does not.

Parameters of the Mark of the Beast

Revelation 13:16 says, "And he causeth all, both small and great, rich and poor, free and bond, to receive a mark in their right hand, or in their foreheads." Notice the word *all*. He, the Antichrist, causes *all*, both small and great to receive the mark. Once again, let's have a quick lesson in Greek. This will surprise you: the word *all* in the Greek language means none other than *all*. The word *every* in the Greek language means none other than *every*. Simple, right? Revelation 13:16 says the beast causes *all* that might buy or sell, *all* great, rich and poor. The parameters of this mark of the beast include a license for life. Those who want to buy food will have to have the mark of the beast; those who want to have water will have to have the mark of the beast. Those wanting shelter and clothing, those who want to keep their heads on their shoulders, in other words, those who want to live, will have to have this famed mark of the beast. The Bible says the Antichrist causes *all* both great and small, slave and free. Social standing will not matter in those days. When the Antichrist arrives, when he comes, when he deceives—the Bible says he will deceive *all*.

Although the mark of the beast is a license for life, it also has a limitation. Keep in mind there are three major series of judgments in the Book of Revelation; there are the famed seven seals, the seven trumpets and the seven vials. At the beginning of the third major judgment an angel comes and pours out the first vial. Revelation 16:1-2 says:

> *And I heard a great voice out of the temple saying to the seven* 61
> *angels, "Go your ways, and pour out the vials of the wrath*
> *of God upon the earth." And the first went, and poured out*
> *his vial upon the earth; and there fell a noisome and grievous*
> *sore upon the men which had the mark of the beast, and upon*
> *them which worshipped his image.*

That which was hidden, that which was stealthy, that which was a deception to all is now a noisome sore! When the Lord shows up with an angel and simply says, "Get rid of it," a grievous sore appears. Now what exactly is a noisome sore? I don't know, but I don't want one! Is the sore so awful that it makes the person scream? Or does the sore actually make a sound? I don't know, but I do know it's not good. The sore causes agony and pain; however, only those who follow the Antichrist and worship him—only those "tares"—will have this sore.

One day the person of the Antichrist will arrive on the scene; he will show up. He will deceive the masses. He will place his mark in the forehead or in the right hand and people will believe they have been given the license to life. Because they possess the mark, they will have the right to buy and sell. But, when the sore of Revelation 16 arrives the proverbial clock runs out. Simultaneously the person of the Antichrist is ready and waiting for the day of the famed Battle of Armageddon—a battle he will fight against Christ.

The Antichrist is a character who will arrive on the scene one day in the future. He will come as one with many answers, yet he will deceive the world. I feel confident in saying that on this very day, this day called today, you do not have to worry whether you will have to receive the mark of the beast. However, I am also absolutely confident in saying that all of us, every one of us, has fallen for his deception. Maybe we have fallen for something that would make us feel good, look good, or something that would somehow make our lives easier, smoother or whatever it may be. When we fall for the devil's deceptions, it gives us a license—a license not to worry about something, a license to feel something, a license to enjoy something. But, do you know what we discover with that license? It has a limitation! One day our rebellion runs its fruition; one day our course of actions will have consequences. And though we don't have to worry today about this famed mark of the beast, what we do have to worry about is the same one who empowers the Antichrist is the same one who tempts us. The same one who will incarnate himself one day during the great tribulation is the same one who whispers in our ears those things contrary to the Word of God. The Israelites during the days of Isaiah wanted to hear counsel that would accommodate their way of life instead of prophecy from the Lord. Isaiah 30:10-11 says, "…Prophecy not unto us right things, speak unto us smooth things, prophecy deceits: Get you out of the way, turn aside out of the path, cause the Holy One of Israel to cease from before us." The Israelites wanted to hear the smooth talking whispers of the evil one rather than heed the truth talking warnings of the Lord. You see, Satan will say, "God said to go right; I think you need to go left. God said to go ahead, but I think you need to stay." His promises are futile and limiting, yet Jesus said, "I will never leave you, I will never forsake you. Come and believe upon Me and your sins will be as far as the east is from the west." And, as prophesied in the Book of Isaiah, He said, "Come and believe upon Me and I will place your sins into the sea of forgetfulness."

Every one of us has the same choice today; it's just a different time. We are not in the tribulation. The Antichrist is not yet in power; however, every one of us has to answer these questions: "Do I believe the promises of Jesus Christ, or do I believe the futile temptations of the devil?" And, we simply need to answer this question: "Whose side are we on?"

Chapter 4

The Battle of Armageddon

Those who chose to receive the Mark of the Beast remain defiant towards God. Under their leader, the Antichrist, they gather themselves at the world's greatest battlefield. There is a multitude of nations and languages spoken, but there is only one purpose -- the last great battle. This clash will determine once and for all who rules the universe. The sky will part. The last trump will sound. Death and destruction will occur as prophesied. A voice from heaven will declare, "It is done." Yet it has just begun, the battle for the universe, the battle of the ages, the battle between good and evil . . . the battle of Armageddon.

As we continue on our journey through the Book of Revelation, keep in mind that although the book seems mysterious at times, the Lord does want us to know and learn from the truth of His Word. As you may recall, we began our study of Revelation in the middle of the book. As we proceed with our study, we will make our way to the end of the Book of Revelation and then we will move to the beginning. In chapters 6 through 19 we examined the seven year event known as the Great Tribulation. During that time period we were introduced to a character known as the Antichrist. Now, we will explore that famous Battle of Armageddon.

There are actually several names in scripture for the place and battle site of Armageddon: the Valley of Jezreel, the Valley of Megiddo, the Valley of Jehoshaphat and the Valley of Armageddon. All four of these names refer to the same place; the same geographical location. For example, the Valley of Jezreel is not a different place than the Valley of Armageddon, it is not an adjacent place; it is the same place. These names are used in various places of scripture to describe the same piece of land. With that being stated, notice what Revelation 16:17-21 says:

> *And the seventh angel poured out his vial into the air; and there came a great voice out of the temple of heaven, from the throne, saying, It is done. And there were voices, and thunders, and lightnings; and there was a great earthquake, and so great. And the great city was divided into three parts, and the cities of the nations fell: and a great Babylon came in remembrance before God, to give unto her the cup of the*

wine of the fierceness of his wrath. And every island fled away, and the mountains were not found. And there fell upon men a great hail out of heaven, every stone about the weight of a talent: and men blasphemed God because of the plague of hail; for the plague thereof was exceeding great.

This is kind of an "earth looking up perspective" of what is occurring at Armageddon. A perspective of Armageddon from Heaven looking down is found in Revelation 19:11-21:

And I saw heaven opened, and behold a white horse; and he that sat upon him was called Faithful and True, and in righteousness he doth judge and make war. His eyes were as a flame of fire, and on his head were many crowns; and he had a name written, that no man knew, but he himself. And he was clothed with a vesture dipped in blood: and his name is called The Word of God. And the armies which were in heaven followed him upon white horses, clothed in fine linen, white and clean. And out of his mouth goeth a sharp sword, that with it he should smite the nations: and he shall rule them with a rod of iron: and he treadeth the winepress of the fierceness and wrath of Almighty God. And he hath on his vesture and on his thigh a name written, KING OF KINGS, AND LORD OF LORDS. And I saw an angel standing in the sun; and he cried with a loud voice, saying to all the fowls that fly in the midst of heaven, Come and gather yourselves together unto the supper of the great God; That you may eat the flesh of kings, and the flesh of captains, and the flesh of mighty men, and the flesh of horses, and of them that sit on them, and the flesh of all men, both free and bond, both small and great. And I

68

saw the beast, and the kings of the earth, and their armies, gathered together to make war against him that sat on the horse, and against his army. And the beast was taken, and with him the false prophet that wrought miracles before him, with which he deceived them that had received the mark of the beast, and them that worshipped his image. These both were cast alive into a lake of fire burning with brimstone. And the remnant were slain with the sword of him that sat upon the horse, which sword proceeded out of his mouth: and all the fowls were filled with their flesh.

The "earth up" or heaven down perspectives in the Book of Revelation give us insight to this last great battle, this last great event that we so commonly know as Armageddon. Most people know and understand that "Armageddon" is not a pleasurable event. The term "Armaged- don" has often been used in an adjectival form such as, "It was an Armageddon experience," or "I'm going to Armageddon." However, Armageddon is a real event; it is the conclusive, final battle of humanity and its rebellion against God.

There is so much information available to us concerning the Book of Revelation and the famed Battle of Armageddon. In fact, unfortunately, some of the so-called information is actually misinformation. So, for a brief moment let us put aside our backgrounds and our expertise in end-time studies, or eschatology, and let us pretend as if we know nothing about the battle of Armageddon. I want to approach this famed battle much like a journalist would with a series of questions involving who, what, when and where and kind of paint a picture of Armageddon.

WHAT IS THE BIG DEAL ABOUT ARMAGEDDON?

Why is there so much talk, study and fascination with Armageddon? In fact, why is Armageddon so important?

A Strategic Location

First, the Valley of Armageddon has an unbelievable strategic location. When you look at a map of the Valley of Armageddon you will notice that it sits in the northern part of what we call Israel. However, it also finds itself in the center of three major continental bodies: Europe, Asia and Africa. You see, in ancient days those kings, princes and queens of royal blood had the resources, money and ability to travel long distances. Common people did not have the ability to travel from one continent to another for two main reasons: 1) they did not have a purpose for doing so, and 2) they did not have the resources. Interestingly enough, there is a road that has been named the Kings Highway. It is a road that leads from Egypt through the Sinai Peninsula and Israel all the way to the area of the Valley of Armageddon.

At the Valley of Armageddon there is a sort of "fork in the road" so-to-speak. Those persons from the Asiatic continent with resources to travel to the land of Egypt would journey west to the Valley of Armageddon and then travel south on the Kings Highway until arriving in Egypt. Persons traveling from Europe to Asia would travel down to the Valley of Armageddon and then proceed eastward until reaching their final destination. The common denominator is this: anyone desiring to travel anywhere had to go through the Valley of Armageddon or travel adjacent to the valley; its location was strategic.

Pictures of the Valley of Armageddon reveal another interesting fact about the area. Images of this valley look as if God Himself took a butter knife out of heaven and just carved the perfect battlefield in the valley. The entire Valley of Armageddon is roughly 1,000 square miles. The true battlefield, the one that is mentioned so vividly in scripture, is a flat plain that looks like the world's largest football field. It is unbelievably flat. If you were to stand on one of the mountainsides and look into the field, you would be amazed. In fact, the land looks so flat that it seems to go on and on for miles on end. To put that number in perspective, that square mileage is the same as Gwinnett County, Rockdale County and Newton County combined. That is massive. Imagine an area or landmass that size, perfectly flat and then imagine

1.5 billion people could fit in the Valley of Armageddon.

that space filled with people who have gathered for a battle. If every person "fighting" on the battlefield in this famous battle was given one square yard, nine square feet of space, 1.5 billion people could fit in the Valley of Armageddon. Now, that is incredible. The flat part, or battlefield, literally disappears into the horizon; it stretches farther than your eye can see. If you were to include the entire Valley of Armageddon with the hills (and by the way, the hills over there are kind of like the hills out in west Texas; they are more like speed bumps so-to-speak), you could put 3.5 billion people within the area. And on top of that, people would have enough space to extend their arms and move around in a full circle. In other words, I am not saying that 3.5 billion people would be packed into the Valley of Armageddon like sardines, standing shoulder to shoulder with no wiggle room. The place is massive! Its strategic location and its geographical size make it a perfect place for a military battle. However, the Valley of Armageddon is not just important because it is militarily strategic; it also has a phenomenal historical significance.

A Historical Significance

Incredible historic events have occurred in this valley. Allow me to describe some of the militarily significant events that have happened in Armageddon. First, there was a prophet of God by the name of Elijah. On one particular day he finds himself on Mount Carmel, just adjacent to this great valley. He is debating against 450 Baal worshippers. The debate is over whose god is the real, one true God. In 1 Kings 18:21-24 Elijah said:

> *How long halt ye between two opinions? If the Lord be God, follow him: but if Baal, then follow him. And the people answered him not a word. Then said Elijah unto the people, I, even I only, remain a prophet of the Lord, but Baal's prophets are four hundred and fifty men. Let them therefore give us two bullocks; and let them choose one bullock for themselves, and cut it in pieces, and lay it on wood, and put no fire under; and I will dress the other bullock, and lay it on wood, and put no fire under: And call ye on the name of your gods, and I will call on the name of the Lord: and the God that answereth by fire, let him be God. And all the people answered and said, It is well spoken.*

72

The 450 Baal worshippers called out to their god. They proceed to cut themselves, they cry, they scream and chant, but to no avail. Elijah, however, calls upon the Lord and fire comes down from heaven and consumes the sacrifice he prepared. After that, he tracks down a woman named Jezebel (I'm pretty sure none of you name your daughters after this woman), and he has her killed in the Valley of Armageddon.

Another historic event involved Solomon, a man whom the Bible calls wiser than any other man. Solomon sets up his northernmost fortress on the south side of the valley—on Megiddo hill where he placed over 450 horses. Why is this significant? Modern-day Lebanon, Syria and Jordan (in biblical terms Gog and Magog) are north of the valley. The Bible says one day in the future people from these places will descend down upon the people of Israel. In order to have a defense against such an attack, you would need to possess that Megiddo hill where Solomon established himself.

In the Valley of Armageddon Gideon took an army from 30,000 men down to 300 men and whipped all of the Midianites in the area. In the Valley of Armageddon, Saul fell and was killed on his sword while battling with the Philistines. This is also the place where Deborah, the famed judge, whipped up on all the boys in that Old Testament story found in the Book of Judges. However, more important than all of that is this: just across the Valley of Armageddon is a small hill that had a small city in days gone past. In that small city is a little town called Nazareth. In this town of Nazareth, on the edge of the Valley of Armageddon, Jesus Christ was raised and reared. It was there where Jesus disclosed to the world that He is the Messiah who had come to save us from our sins. When Jesus was 12 years of age he went down to Jerusalem for the Passover Feast. In fact, He went to Jerusalem on a regular basis and in order to do so, He either had to walk adjacent to or through the Valley of Armageddon. On a regular basis, Jesus

Christ walked the very dirt that, according to Revelation 19, He will one day claim; the valley which is rightfully and dutifully His.

WHEN WILL ARMAGEDDON TAKE PLACE?

The size and grandeur of the battlefield in the Valley of Armageddon is interesting. The historical significance is fascinating. But, don't we all want to know *when* the Battle of Armageddon will take place?

Bear in mind that the Battle of Armageddon actually takes place at the conclusion, at the end of the tribulation, that seven year time period described in Revelation 6 through Revelation 19. In fact, in Revelation 16:17 says, "And the seventh angel poured out his vial into the air; and there came a great voice out of the temple of heaven, from the throne, saying, It is done." This is the end of the end. It is the very last thing in what we know as the time of the Great Tribulation. The Battle of Armageddon is also the time when Jesus Christ returns, as Revelation 19 describes. You may be thinking, "What about Revelation 17 and 18?" Well, those chapters describe what happens to Babylon and the other entities mentioned in Revelation 16. Know this: the Battle of Armageddon occurs at the end of the Great Tribulation and at the second coming of Jesus Christ.

You may have seen a bumper sticker or t-shirt with the saying, "Jesus Christ is coming back and boy is He mad." That is a somewhat humorous approach to a literal event. Understand what has happened before Jesus Christ returns: the judgments of God! The sun has turned colors, the moon has turned colors, people have died, all kind of disease and famine have occurred, the water has turned to blood—and then, just when it seems things could not get any worse—the King of Kings

74

and the Lord of Lords returns! And, keep this in mind, He is taking no prisoners! You see, at the end of the Great Tribulation, the battle occurs. At the return of Jesus Christ, the battle begins.

WHO IS AT THE BATTLE OF ARMAGEDDON?

Now that we have determined when the Battle of Armageddon will occur, let us examine scripture to discover who will be at the battle. Revelation 19:19 says, "And I saw the beast, and the kings of the earth, and their armies, gathered together to make war against him that sat on the horse, and against his army." All of humanity is gathered there; all of the kings and their armies. A second group of people will also be present at this great battle. Revelation 19:14 says, "And the armies which were in heaven followed him upon white horses, clothed in fine linen, white and clean." At the moment of this battle, all of those who have believed on Jesus, all of those who have claimed they were sinners and they needed Jesus to save them are with Jesus Christ at this moment. This includes the Church of believers, the raptured ones, the Old Testament saints, the tribulation saints and the angels. They will all follow Jesus Christ to this battle. Those who have rebelled against God, all of humanity who have thumbed their noses at God, all of humanity who have said, "I will not repent of my sins, I will not turn to Jesus, I can do it on my own" will be on the battlefield.

But, how can so many people fit on the battlefield of Armageddon? Well, allow me to take a stab at answering that question. Consider that the earth's current population is around 7 billion people. When the fourth seal is opened, one-third of humanity is killed. Sometime later a trumpet judgment occurs, and one-fourth of humanity is killed. Keep in mind also, that water turns to blood and because of that, many men died. The Valley of Armageddon can hold approximately four billion people; so when the Bible says all of humanity is there that is what it means. All of humanity is there; every individual, small and great, free and bond who has rejected the truth of Jesus Christ shows up to this place for one final showdown. Remember too, that those who have believed on Jesus Christ have followed Him from heaven to this great battle. This is the battle of all battles. The regiments of angels are getting together, everybody is there!

Revelation 19:19 also tells us that the beast was there, the false prophet was there, and I surmise that every demonic entity known to the universe is at the Battle of Armageddon. Trust me, when Armageddon takes place you won't need CNN coverage; you won't need FOX coverage; everyone will be there to witness this event live! Everyone who takes part in this event will be within visual sight of the happenings.

76

So, this place—this Valley of Armageddon is strategic, it's historical. The battle takes place at the end of the Great Tribulation and the coming of Christ and everyone is there. So, what actually happens?

WHAT HAPPENS AT THE BATTLE OF ARMAGEDDON?
Revelation 16:18 says, "And there were voices, and thunders, and lightnings; and there was a great earthquake, such as was not since men were upon the earth, so mighty an earthquake, and so great." Absolute total destruction happens at the Battle of Armageddon. When the sixth seal is opened in Revelation 6, the Bible tells us that there will be an earthquake of such magnitude that all of the mountains and islands will shake. Revelation 16:20 says, "And every island fled away, and the mountains were not found." All of us have seen the devastation

of an enormous earthquake. Buildings and structures are annihilated; what was once there is no longer and what we didn't know was there shows up. Earthquakes are horrific. But, imagine an earthquake of such magnitude that every mountain is flattened and every island is gone! Isaiah prophecies this event in Isaiah 40:4 when he is speaks of John the Baptist's ministry coming before Jesus: "Every valley shall be exalted, and every mountain and hill shall be made low: and the crooked shall be made straight, and the rough places plain." When Jesus the Messiah comes to reign, the crooked with be made straight and the high will be made low.

But how does the earthquake of Revelation 16 occur? The Bible tells us when Jesus actually touches his foot at the Mount of Olives, a cavern is created all the way to what we know as the Valley of Armageddon. Basically, when the King of Kings and Lord of Lords shows up and steps foot on the ground, the whole earth is forever changed; mountains are taken down and islands are gone—it is an incredible devastation!

Can you imagine what would happen to the militaries of the world if an earthquake like this occurred? Tanks will no longer work, planes will be broken and fuel will be deposited along the earth creating fires. The Battle of Armageddon takes place, not with military equipment, but with sticks and stones. Some may laugh at this image, saying that the Bible must be antiquated. However, think about the countries that have suffered major earthquakes—the equipment that once operated well is no longer in working order after a devastating earthquake. At the Battle of Armageddon, after the greatest earthquake of all, there will be nothing left with which to fight Jesus—except a rock! Israel is full of rocks! There are rocks everywhere, and there are rocks all over

Simple

the Valley of Armageddon. The enemies of Jesus Christ will be so upset and mad at the devastation, that they will be willing to pick up a rock to fight the King of Kings and Lord of Lords.

Wide-spread death will also be prevalent during the Battle of Armageddon. In fact, Revelation 14:20 is a fulfillment of the prophecy found in Isaiah 63:3 that says:

I have trodden the winepress alone; and of the people there was none with me: for I will tread them in mine anger, and trample them in my fury; and their blood shall be sprinkled upon my garments, and I will stain all my raiment.

Millions upon millions upon billions of people are being slaughtered by the King of Kings and Lord of Lords and yet, the last man left standing still believes that he can defeat Jesus.

78

The Lord's judgment comes to its full fruition when He returns. Revelation 14:20 speaks of the bloodshed that will occur during the Battle of Armageddon: "And the winepress was trodden without the city, and blood came out of the winepress, even unto the horse bridles, by the space of a thousand and six hundred furlongs." At the Battle of Armageddon, the blood of those who fight against Jesus will be as high as the horse's bridle. Keep in mind the vast land mass that makes up the Valley of Armageddon; some say the area is about 180 miles in length. Incidentally, from the edge of the Valley of Armageddon to Jerusalem down the Jordan River Valley is 180 miles. Picture this, all of humanity fighting against Jesus is funneling into this valley, one after one, platoon after platoon, million after million are slain to such a magnitude that the blood rises to the bridle of a horse and stretches a length of 180 miles.

Understand this, the blood runs deep. There is mass destruction and tremendous loss of life.

WHY DOES ARMAGEDDON OCCUR?

First, Armageddon happens because it is the last final rebellion of mankind. The Antichrist, his demons and his followers are there for one reason and one reason only: they want to fight the King of Kings and Lord of Lords face to face. This is their last chance to contend for power.

I am reminded of one of my favorite stories in the Bible; the story of Samson. Now Samson, the guy with the long dreadlocks, was given strength and power as long as he never cut his hair. No matter who he came against, he could whip him. In fact, in one particular story, he takes the jawbone of a donkey and kills one thousand men in a battle. The reason I like this story so much is because it literally reveals 79
the stupidity of humanity. While Samson was killing each man, one after one after one, what did the other men think? "Oh, he has already killed 500 men, but I can take him." What did that last man think, after 999 men were already dead, did he really think he could defeat Samson? This is how I picture the Battle of Armageddon. Millions upon millions upon billions of people are being slaughtered by the King of Kings and Lord of Lords and yet, the last man left standing still believes that he can defeat Jesus.

Revelation 16 reminds us that men blasphemed God. Armageddon is that final picture of what happens when we let sin take control of our lives. At first, sin seems like a good idea. Sometimes it just seems like something that is an inconvenience, but yet it feels good. But, eventually we get so consumed with sin that we will do whatever it takes to eliminate God out of our lives so that we can run and rule our lives.

You see, here we are looking at the Battle of Armageddon—a picture of what sin ultimately produces. Sin produces that mentality that no matter how bad it looks, we can still go ahead and fight against God and do whatever we want to do. Armageddon happens because we don't want anyone, particularly God, telling us how to live our lives.

Understand this, the Battle of Armageddon happens because of humanity's rebellion, but it is also God's grand finale. Recently I spoke with a man in my church who was saved "later" in life. He was in his late thirties or early forties before he entered into a relationship with Jesus Christ. Statistically speaking, that is kind of late in life. He mentioned to me the fact that God has so much patience. He said, "I can't believe that God put up with me for so long. If I were God, I would not have put up with me. I just don't understand how God has so much patience. How does He put up with so much? He sees so much rebellion and yet it's as if He doesn't do anything about it."

God's patience will wear out one day! All of the rebellion of humanity, all of the thumbing our noses at God and all of the prideful attitudes of "I don't need you, Jesus—I want to do it my way" will come to a head! God is going to reach that limit and it will all be over. When Armageddon commences, everyone who rebels against Jesus Christ is defeated and destroyed. Death ensues. Understand this: everyone who fights against Jesus Christ will lose. This battle is God's grand finale, and He will show the world, "I am the King of Kings. I am the Lord of Lords."

You see, no matter who you are or what you do or what you hide, eventually it all comes out. We are masters of deceit. We are masters of putting up an illusion. We are masters of putting up a persona, convincing ourselves that no one, nowhere, no how will there be anyone ever find out who I really am or what I am really doing. At the Valley of Armageddon you discover whose army you are in. Everyone at Armageddon is in the army: you are either enlisted in the army of Jesus Christ or you are in the army of the Antichrist. One that day it will be disclosed where one's true allegiance lies. According to the Bible, all of humanity will be present at that Battle of Armageddon—all of humanity and all of the heavens are there! The only question you need to answer today is this: on which side will you be fighting? You will be on one of those sides. Will you be fighting against Jesus or with Him? The results are dramatically different.

Chapter 5

The Millennium

The Battle of Armageddon has come to completion. There is a new order to the universe. The old ruler, Satan, is bound with his demons. The new ruler, Jesus Christ, reigns from a throne in Jerusalem. It is a time that humanity has dreamed of for ages. There is actual world peace. There is no hunger, want, or need. There is no death or destruction. It is a time like no other. It is not a dream. It is not fantasy. It is ... the Millennium.

The subject matter in this chapter is not the most controversial in the book Revelation, but it is at the center of the controversy. All views regarding the chronology of Revelation (they will be discussed in further detail later in this chapter) build their "cases" or perspectives around seven simple verses in Revelation chapter 20. Before we delineate these varying views, let us explore what they all have in common.

First, all views regarding the book of Revelation agree that humanity and the "world" has a sin problem. This problem initiated in the Garden of Eden has not been eradicated to this date or during the events of the book of Revelation. All views believe that Jesus Christ is the answer to the problem of sin; they just disagree on when Jesus actually removes sin, not from the heart of a repentant soul, but from the earth permanently.

85

Second, all major views concerning the book of Revelation believe that Jesus Christ is going to return to earth. They disagree often on the manner and timing, but all agree that the return of Jesus Christ is going to happen. Additionally, they believe that at His return He will be visible. Along with the physical and visible return of Jesus is the affirmation that those who choose to not only reject the salvation message of Jesus, but also "fight against" Him are ultimately punished. Third, the subject matters following Revelation chapter 20 and the millennium: judgment, eternity, new Heaven and the new earth are surprisingly well agreed on by even those who completely disagree on the timing of the millennium in reference to Jesus' second coming. Therefore, to summarize the "agreements," those who completely disagree on timing and length all agree on the curse of sin, the physical return of Jesus, and a future blissful and rewarding eternity for those who have become born again through Jesus Christ. Now, for that which divides.

The term millennium has caused great controversy, but when we look at the concept of the millennium through the Word of God, it will cause great comfort in every one of our lives. By strict definition the word millennium means a thousand years. The passage of scripture in the Book of Revelation chapter 20 describing the millennium is small in nature, only seven verses, though it is prophesied in Psalms, Isaiah and other prophetic books. Almost every perspective, every theology, every attitude toward the Book of Revelation is based in relationship to this small passage of scripture.

86 Revelation 20:1-7 states:

And I saw an angel come down from heaven, having the key of the bottomless pit and a great chain in his hand. And he laid hold on the dragon, that old serpent, which is the Devil, and Satan, and bound him a thousand years, And cast him into the bottomless pit, and shut him up, and set a seal upon him, that he should deceive the nations no more, till the thousand years should be fulfilled: and after that he must be loosed a little season. And I saw thrones, and they sat upon them, and judgment was given unto them: and I saw the souls of them that were beheaded for the witness of Jesus, and for the word of God, and which had not worshipped the beast, neither his image, neither had received his mark upon their foreheads, or in their hands; and they lived and reigned with Christ a thousand years. But the rest of the dead lived not again until the thousand years were finished. This is the first resurrection. Blessed and holy is he that hath part in the first resurrection: on such the second death hath no power, but they shall be priests of God and of Christ, and shall reign with him a thousand years. And when the thousand years are expired, Satan shall be loosed out of his prison.

Notice that there are six specific references to the term "a thousand years," hence the term millennium.

WHAT IS THE MILLENNIUM?

The millennium is the desired time period of all of humanity. We joke about beauty contestants answering every question with the words "world peace." Every country, whether it has a benevolent leader or much the opposite, at least in formal political rhetoric, claims that it desires world peace. Currently the whole world resides in a "world of pieces," but according to Revelation chapter 20 there is a day of world peace coming. However, this day will look very different from how the world envisions, pictures, or tries to create it.

A Desired Time

We live in a world today of much hostility. There are people, both on this side of the Atlantic and the other side of the Atlantic, that are postulating, particularly in the Middle East, that if we just change the borders, if we just change the way things are situated, that will bring peace. Let me give you a headline that you will not find in the news: no matter what the summit is, no matter who the leaders are, there is no world peace until Revelation chapter 20 comes to pass. Leaders can talk rhetoric, they can change the borders in regard to Israel (though it is not right to do so), but it will not bring the peace that they desire. Everyone wants peace. Famous institutions and organizations quote from Isaiah chapter 11 that prophesies that there is a day coming when people will beat their swords into ploughshares. Weapons used to kill other people will actually become instruments of harvest. Isaiah prophesies that one day the wolf will lie down with the lamb, children will literally play with snakes and serpents. It is a time like none other, and this is the time of peace that everyone desires.

A Distinct Time

The millennium is also a very distinct time. Revelation 20:1-7 says "a thousand years" six times in seven verses. I recognize that I am not the brightest bulb in the chandelier. I recognize that sometimes I do not always have a full set of French fries in my Happy Meal, but sometimes the Lord makes it so abundantly clear that we would have to have our heads in the sand not to understand what He is saying. When the Lord says something six times in seven verses, that's called a spiritual two by four. In other words, God says, for those of you who are not paying attention—thump! Pay attention! His repetition should get our attention.

> *That is what the millennium is; it is everything humanity has always wanted.*

88

The millennium is a distinct time period like none other. It is a time period when, according to the Word of God, Satan is bound. It is a time period when temptation does not come from Satan's throne. It is a time when Jesus literally, physically, reigns from a throne in Jerusalem, in the country of Israel surrounded by the twelve tribes and His witnesses. I know that scenario is not politically correct, but it is biblical. It is a distinct time period where those who have placed their faith in Jesus Christ will reign with Him. That is what the millennium is; it is everything humanity has always wanted.

WHEN WILL THE MILLENNIUM OCCUR?

Many people often wonder when the millennium will occur. The overwhelming majority of people who study the Book of Revelation, whether they know it or not, will fall into one of three "camps" of theology: pre-millennial, a-millennial or post-millennial.

The words "post", "a", or "pre" refer to the time period of Christ's return in relationship to the time of His millennial reign. For example, post-millennial, by the word, means that the millennium will occur and then Jesus will return to earth (Jesus' return is post-millennial). The ideology here is that the church of Jesus Christ, those who are believers, those who are saved will do such a good job in propagating the gospel of Jesus that sin will be eradicated, righteousness will take over, and such a euphoria will be created that Jesus will have to come back. This was the dominating view until World War I took place. Until that time we thought everything was getting better and that everything was headed toward a utopian world. There are those who still claim this belief; however, they are few in number.

A-millennialism means "no millennium." (The letter "a" in Greek means "not.") Even though the millennium is mentioned six times in seven verses, a-millennialists believe that the millennium is not literal. They believe the Book of Revelation is to be as symbolic—more of an allegory, or a story of the battle of good versus evil. A-millenialists adhere to the idea that there will be some good times and there will be some bad times, and they refuse the idea that there is one great time where Satan is bound because they believe that he was bound at the time of the cross.

I unashamedly fall into the pre-millennial perspective, which basically states that Jesus Christ will return prior to the millennial time period on earth. The Bible states that according to 2 Timothy 4 the world will get worse and worse, sin will overtake more and more, until Jesus comes back at the end of the tribulation known as Armageddon, where He destroys those that are His enemies and sets up His kingdom. Armageddon is described in Revelation chapter 19 and the millennium is described in Revelation chapter 20. Speaking from a biblical perspective, based on the Book of Revelation, I believe the millennium happens after Armageddon when sin and the devil are eradicated.

Those of you who are Christ-followers understand that there was a point in your life when you admitted and accepted that you are a sinner and that you need to be forgiven of your sins. Upon that realization you humbled yourself before the cross of Jesus Christ and said, "I cannot save myself. I am not smart enough. I am not good enough. You paid the penalty for my sin on the cross because I cannot do it." According to the Word of God you entered what is known as the Kingdom of God. The Bible says your body became the temple of the Holy Spirit. You became born again; you became a new creation. At the point of salvation Jesus Christ immediately lives and reigns in your life. You see, even if Jesus is not physically living and reigning from a throne in Jerusalem, He still reigns in your life. Understand that the millennium is a contrast from salvation. Salvation is when, in the midst of a sinful world, we ask a Savior to mercifully save us; the millennium is when that Savior establishes His physical, literal throne, and those who have claimed and professed Him as Savior will reign with Him for 1,000 years—that distinct period of time known as the millennium. However, as Christians we do not have to wait until the millennium in order for Jesus Christ to reign. Understand that Jesus reigns in your life at salvation, and He will physically reign on a throne during the millennium.

WHY IS THE MILLENNIUM SO IMPORTANT?

So, why is the study of the millennium so important? The first thing we need to know is this: the millennium "fixes" the protocol problem that we have on earth. According to 2 Corinthians 4:4 Satan is called the god of this world, the prince of darkness. There are passages that teach how he wreaks havoc, day in and day out, on those who follow Jesus Christ. Though he wreaks havoc, though he runs around, torments and tempts, there is coming a day when Jesus Christ Himself "fixes" that problem. You see, Jesus Christ binds Satan for a thousand years, and He sets up His kingdom and runs the world the way it was designed to be run. He fixes our current protocol problem.

91

The initial area of protocol that Jesus via His Millennial reign "fixes" is the world's concern with and obsession over world peace. The most famous example of the world's belief that humanity can bring about world piece was World War 1. On the 11th hour of the 11th day of the 11th month of November 1918 the famous World War I Armistice was signed. The war that claimed 16 million causalities and 21 million injuries had drawn to a close. In response, the leaders of the world rejoiced and celebrated.

In England David Lloyd George spoke these famous words to the House of Commons, "I hope we may say that thus, this fateful morning, came an end to all wars."

George's famed statement was originally penned by H.G. Wells in 1914 but most famously quoted by Woodrow Wilson following the "Great War." Those 4 years at the beginning of the 20th century were so tragic yet so hopeful. They were tragic because of loss; hopeful because of the thought that the "war to end all wars" had occurred. History and 144 million war-related deaths later the 21st century would dawn with war around every corner. Every "big" war is touted as being the "big one" that will end all others – history has taught us otherwise. The prophet Isaiah, speaking of the millennial reign of Jesus spoke these words:

Peace: Isaiah 11:6-9

> *The wolf also shall dwell with the lamb, and the leopard shall lie down with the kid; and the calf and the young lion and the fatling together; and a little child shall lead them. And the cow and the bear shall feed; their young ones shall lie down together: and the lion shall eat straw like the ox. And the sucking child shall play on the hole of the asp, and the weaned child shall put his hand on the cockatrice' den. They shall not hurt nor destroy in all my holy mountain: for the earth shall be full of the knowledge of the LORD, as the waters cover the sea.*

The world, until the millennial reign of Jesus, will continue to have a peace problem. We will continue to struggle with the causalities and hardships of war. Why? Simply put, sin is a present daily reality.

The "sin factor" is not removed until the Millennium – then and only then will World peace take place.

The second area of protocol that Jesus' reign establishes is that of prosperity. When I use the word "prosperity" I am literally referring to material blessings, but not "materialism." "Material blessings" does not refer to a state of living where one receives more and more and more (this is by definition Materialism). Rather it refers to a state of living where one's basic needs are met and there is no want, physically. This is a promise of the millennium – not only a world in peace, but also a world without want.

Prosperity: Isaiah 35:1-2

> *The wilderness and the solitary place shall be glad for them; and the desert shall rejoice, and blossom as the rose. It shall blossom abundantly, and rejoice even with joy and singing: the glory of Lebanon shall be given unto it, the excellency of Carmel and Sharon, they shall see the glory of the LORD, and the excellency of our God.*

93

Whether your specific heritage is Atlanta, the Appalachian's, or Africa there is a phrase, often connected to material blessings, that is near and dear to everyone reading this: "The American Dream." This phrase means a variety of things to various people, but its original intent is far from its current interpretation. The millennium's idea and version of prosperity differs from the western world's.

The origin of the phrase is a 1931 book by James Truslow Adams entitled *The American Epic*. There are many notable quotes or statements from the book, but here is one of the most fascinating:

> It is not a dream of motor cars and high wages merely, but a dream of social order in which each man and each woman shall be able to attain to the fullest stature of which they are innately capable, and be recognized by others for what they are, regardless of the fortuitous circumstances of birth or position.

Yes, the American dream is achievement and "success" regardless of race, background, birth, or position, but the "Dream" has taken on a whole new life in recent decades. It has become a "dream" of more, more, and still more (Materialism). We have become a culture, even in the church, that believes that the blessings of life, even those from God come in and are realized in the form of material items, "stuff."

The millennium brings about not a "dream" or "materialism" but rather true Biblical prosperity.

The American Dream never meant, "he who dies with the most toys wins," but that has become its bumper sticker. What Adams meant in his book was that ability and desire, not things and "stuff," were to be desired. The millennium brings about not a "dream" or "materialism" but rather true Biblical prosperity. During the millennial reign of Jesus Christ this prosperity will include the Biblical definition and realization of material blessings.

The third "protocol" that Jesus "fixes" during the Millennium is humanity's physical health. Worldwide, but particularly in the United States, there is an ever growing concern with and near obsession with physical health and "healthcare." Politicians are divided and the country

94

is divided on whom, how much, or what determines the necessary minimum that one is entitled to in regard to our health. However, there is one underlying theme of the entire discussion – everyone (those on "both sides of the isle) believes that humanity is not in the health it should be or deserves to be.

Literally, billions and billions of dollars are spent each year on necessary and elective healthcare treatments. When doctors do not give diagnosis and recommendations desired by the patients they often elect to go "elsewhere" for treatment. It seems that humanity will spare no cost or length to "get well." Humanity's ailing bodies are a by-product of the fall of humanity. When sin entered the world so did death. The process toward death naturally involves sickness and health issues. The millennial reign of Jesus not only addresses these concerns but also solves them.

95

Physical health: Isaiah 65:20
There shall be no more thence an infant of days, nor an old man that hath not filled his days: for the child shall die an hundred years old; but the sinner being an hundred years old shall be accursed.

The millennium does not just fix the protocol problem; it fulfills a very important prophecy. The great prophets of the Bible prophesied that the millennium time period would come to fruition. Jesus also spoke, or prophesied, about the millennium in Matthew 26. When Jesus addresses the disciples in Matthew 26, He is just a few hours from the betrayal, His arrest, and His unfair trial. In fact, the words He delivers in Matthew 26 are probably spoken within twelve hours of His cruel crucifixion—when He was placed upon a cross for the world to see. Matthew 26 is that portion of scripture where we receive guidance to participate in the Lord's Supper. It is a time when the bread is consumed; it is a time when the juice is consumed. Notice what Jesus says in Matthew 26:27-29:

> *And he (Jesus) took the cup, and gave thanks, and gave it to them, saying, Drink you all of it; For this is my blood of the new testament, which is shed for many for the remission of sins. But I say unto you, I will not drink henceforth of this fruit of the vine, until that day when I drink it new with you in my Father's kingdom."*

Jesus prophesies and declares at the Last Supper the same message spoken by the Old Testament prophets—one day He will physically reign as King of Kings. You see, those people alive during the days of Christ expected a Messiah to come on the scene in the role of a majestic, powerful, authoritative king. We understand that Jesus Christ came to earth in humble means—much different from what the world expected and desired. At the Last Supper, when Jesus broke bread with His disciples, He declared that all of the prophecy that the people wanted Him to fulfill at His first coming will occur at the time of the millennium; it will happen. He will dwell with you and me much like the Lord dwelt with Adam and Eve in the Garden of Eden; He walked with them in the cool of the day. The Bible says that Jesus will eat, drink, consume and dwell with us in His Father's Kingdom—a millennial kingdom will be established, and we will see Jesus reign in His role as the King.

When Jesus arose from the dead, He spent roughly forty days with His disciples pouring into them and teaching them and then He ascended into heaven to sit at the right hand of the Father, always making intercession for us. The Bible says that when that ascension event occurred the disciples wondered if that was the time when Jesus would restore the kingdom. In other words, would this be the time when Jesus Christ established His physical, literal throne on earth. Jesus told His disciples, "That is not for you to know, just hold on because the Holy Spirit is going to come upon you and you will be My witnesses in Jerusalem, Judea, Samaria and the uttermost parts of the earth." You see, the millennial reign is such a vital concept in scripture that Jesus mentioned it last at the Lord's Supper, the disciples mentioned it last before His ascension, and it just so happens that in Revelation chapter 20 of the last book of the Bible we are told that one day the Father's Kingdom on earth will occur.   97

When we partake of the Lord's Supper we are claiming that one day we will partake of this supper with Christ in person. Job made this statement in the Old Testament: "One day I will stand on the earth with my Redeemer." Yes, the Lord's Supper is a celebration of the past, but it is also a celebration of the future—God is not done and He will bring to fruition what He has prophesied for millennia about the millennium.

Chapter 6

Judgment Day

The universe's final chapter comes to a close with the dissolving of the heavens and the earth. All of humanity assembles itself before a throne. A voice speaks and books are opened. Lives are examined and destinations are determined. This is the final moment for all of creation. Eternity is in the balance. There is no turning back. The future has been decided. This is the day everyone has heard about. This is the day that everyone gives an account. This is . . . Judgment Day

Interestingly enough, every religion, every philosophy, and every human being ultimately answers the question about that one fatal, final day known as Judgment Day. There are literally myriads of perspectives about this concept, but what does the Word of God say about this event and how must we, each and every one of us, respond to God in light of Judgment Day?

It is significant to note that there are various judgments in scripture. Matthew 25 talks about the judgment of the nations. The Bible speaks about our sins being judged. In 2 Corinthians 5:10 it says that Christians must stand before the judgment seat of Christ. Revelation 20 says that God is seated on a great white throne. Oftentimes Judgment Day is called the Great White Throne Judgment. Revelation 20 beginning in verse 7 follows on the heels of the millennium. Revelation 20:7-15 states:

101

> *And when the thousand years are expired, Satan shall be loosed out of his prison, And shall go out to deceive the nations which are in the four quarters of the earth, Gog, and Magog, to gather them together to battle: the number of whom is as the sand of the sea. And they went up on the breadth of the earth, and compassed the camp of the saints about, and the beloved city: and fire came down from God out of heaven, and devoured them. And the devil that deceived them was cast into the lake of fire and brimstone, where the beast and the false prophet are, and shall be tormented day and night for ever and ever. And I saw a great white throne, and him that sat on it, from whose face the earth and the heaven fled*

away; and there was found no place for them. And I saw the dead, small and great, stand before God; and the books were opened: and another book was opened, which is the book of life: and the dead were judged out of those things which were written in the books, according to their works. And the sea gave up the dead which were in it; and death and hell delivered up the dead which were in them: and they were judged every man according to their works. And death and hell were cast into the lake of fire. This is the second death. And whosoever was not found written in the book of life was cast into the lake of fire.

> *So, the proper question is not to ask who is present. The question we need to ask about Judgment Day is who is actually judged?*

102

The concept of Judgment Day, this idea that every human being will one day stand face-to-face before God, has so many different controversial opinions, perspectives and ideas. Unfortunately, if you go get two books about the topic of Judgment Day, you are probably going to get three different opinions. So, I want to approach the concept of Judgment Day as if we have never studied it, never looked at it or never done a Bible study on it by answering those most basic and simplistic questions: who, what , when, where, why and how.

WHO IS JUDGED AT JUDGMENT DAY?

Notice the question before you. The question is not who is at Judgment Day, for as you read through Revelation 20, you will discover that the "who" present at Judgment Day is every entity that has ever existed. First and foremost, God Almighty is there. The Bible speaks to the fact that the cherubim are there, the seraphim are there and all the angelic hosts are there. All of those who have believed in God through Jesus Christ are there—the Old Testament saints, the "church age" saints, those that endured the tribulation time period, those who made it through the millennium time period, everyone who has claimed the name of Jesus Christ, everyone who would be identified on the right-hand of the Father, and angelic beings. On the other side of the equation, the devil himself is there, the Antichrist is there, the false prophet is there, the demons and principalities are there, the powers are there, and everyone who has looked into the face of God and rejected and rebelled against Him. Everyone is there—both those who believe and those who do not believe.

So, the proper question is not to ask who is present. The question we need to ask about Judgment Day is who is actually *judged?* You will notice that Revelation 20:12 says, "I saw the dead, small and great, stand before God." So, those judged at Judgment Day are the sinners who are resurrected of the dead. Revelation 20:4-5 says:

> *And I saw thrones, and they sat upon them, and judgment was given unto them: and I saw the souls of them that were beheaded for the witness of Jesus, and for the word of God, and which had not worshipped the beast, neither his image, neither had received his mark upon their foreheads, or in their hands; and they lived and reigned with Christ a thousand years. But the rest of the dead lived not again until the thousand years were finished. This is the first resurrection.*

On Judgment Day, the Bible says those that were dead are judged according to their works. The Bible tells me in Ephesians 2:1 that you

103

and I, all of us, before we came to know Jesus Christ as our personal Savior, before we confessed that we were sinners and asked Him to save us and forgive us, that we were dead in our trespasses and in our sins. One of the most simplistic verses of scripture is found in 1 John 5:12. It says whoever believes in the Son has life and whoever does not believe in the Son does not have life.

Notice there is a distinction made in Revelation 20: there are those who are found in the books and their works are examined and then there is that famous Book of Life. I think what is important to note is this: who is judged on this fatal, famous Judgment Day are not those who have been resurrected *from* the dead, but those who have been resurrected *of* the dead.

104 According to Ephesians 2:1, as well as other passages, a person can be alive and breathing, but if a person has sin in his life and has not asked Jesus to save him and forgive him then he is a walking dead man. When a person says, "Jesus, I'm a sinner, save me," then the Bible says that person is resurrected *from* the dead instantly. According to Revelation 20:4-5 these are not those who are resurrected *from* the dead; this is the resurrection of the dead. It is at this time when all of those who died in their sins without asking God to forgive them through Jesus Christ are resurrected and brought up to judgment.

WHAT HAPPENS AT JUDGMENT DAY?

I want to profess to you that Judgment Day is not so much a time of judgment as it is a time of sentencing. Notice that the Bible says they stood before a great white throne. The word *judging* is not actually insinuated. In fact, what we discover in Revelation 20 is that a separation has already occurred. The Bible makes it very clear who is on the Lord's side and who is not. Jesus prophesied in Matthew 25 there would be those on His right hand who would go to everlasting life; those on His left hand would go into the lake of fire prepared for the devil and his angels. Understand that throughout scripture, there is a very clear line drawn between those who believe and those who do not. In John 3:36 Jesus makes the statement that those who do not believe are already condemned. Before Judgment Day a separation between those who believe and those who do not believe has already occurred. Whether people are alive and breathing on planet earth or whether they have already passed into what we would call eternity—a separation between believers and unbelievers has already been made.

Revelation 20 tells us that there are three entities that give up their dead: death, hell, and the sea. Most of us understand the concepts of death and hell and how those entities can give up their dead, but understand the meaning of the sea is a little more difficult. I have had the privilege of going to the Holy Land, to the land of Israel. On one particular day I had the privilege of being on the Sea of Galilee. In scripture the Sea of Galilee is also known as the Lake of Gennesaret. This body of water is known both as a lake and a sea. Interestingly enough, Satan and his demons are sent to the lake of fire. I believe the Bible is teaching us that no one who has rejected God through Jesus Christ will escape Judgment Day. When death gives up its dead, hell gives up its dead and the sea gives up its dead every person who has ever rejected Christ will be gathered and brought to Judgment Day. No matter what age they have lived in, no matter where they have been, or what stature they were, the Bible says whomever rejected Christ is brought before the judgment, and they are not "condemned" as much as they are "sentenced."

You have seen it on television, and unfortunately most of us have seen it happen to a friend or loved one—an individual commits a crime and is condemned as guilty of that crime. As soon as he is pronounced guilty, the jury says he is guilty, the judge determines that he is guilty, typically that individual goes into incarceration and is brought back at a different time to be sentenced.

In Revelation 20 the picture that we get of Judgment Day is that everyone who is presented has already been condemned to an eternity apart from God; everyone has been condemned to the lake of fire but has yet to be sentenced. That is why Revelation 20:14 calls it the second death. When one physically dies without Christ in his life, then that is the first death. The second death is when the sentence takes place for all of eternity. Those who have rejected Christ will be present at judgment day, where the final sentence upon their eternal life is declared. Guilt has been pronounced earlier, but the sentencing takes place at Judgment Day.

Those who have rejected Christ will be present at judgment day, where the final sentence upon their eternal life is declared.

WHEN DOES JUDGMENT DAY OCCUR?

So we have answered the "who" question, and we have answered the "what" question. Now we need to answer the question when does judgment day occur? Judgment day is actually "sandwiched" in time. Let me give you a practical, daily example. My wife and I pack our boys' school lunches on a regular basis, and we typically make the famous PB and J. You take peanut butter, you take jelly and you "sandwich" them between two pieces of bread. That is what we call a sandwich. We are not real smart; we are just very practical when we name things. So, we understand that a sandwich is that which is "in-between" two other things. The same thing happens in Revelation 20.

You may have noticed that Revelation 20:7 mentions that Satan is loosed, or set free, for a season. Gog and Magog are mentioned. The millennium, a thousand years of Jesus Christ reigning on the throne from Jerusalem—a time of peace and prosperity, a time when everything humanity has ever wanted and always desired—is transpiring, but at the end of that thousand years the devil is let loose for a season. What this confirms to us is something very clear: it does not matter when or where a person lives, everyone ultimately has to 107 make a decision for Jesus Christ. During the millennial time period people are born. Satan is bound, there is no temptation, there is no opportunity to reject the things of Jesus Christ; however, *every* person has to make a decision. Do we choose the world or do we choose the Word? Do we choose the devil or do we choose Jesus? Everybody ultimately has to choose.

When Satan is loosed the Battle of Gog and Magog ensues. (Gog and Magog is modern southern Russia or Turkey.) The army of Satan comes in from the north to Jerusalem where Jesus is reigning. Notice that there are no white horses, no swords, no crowns, no battle that takes place. In fact, in this final rebellion notice what God does: He just calls fire down from heaven and it is over—Satan and his army is condemned at that point.

Revelation 21 says, "And I saw a new heaven and a new earth and a New Jerusalem. The former things are passed away; there are no more tears, no more heartache. The "when" of Judgment Day is this: it is sandwiched between the last great rebellion and eternity. The judgment is the last event in the realm of time as we know it.

WHERE DOES JUDGMENT DAY OCCUR?

We know who is going to be judged. We know that a sentencing takes place. We know the judgment happens during the last great earthly rebellion and eternity. So, the next valid question to ask would be this: where does it occur? Revelation 20:11 says, "And I saw a great white throne, and him that sat on it, from whose face the earth and the heaven fled away." Interestingly enough, we cannot attach a specific geographical location to the event of the final judgment, 108 the Great White Throne Judgment. In fact, the closest longitude and latitude readings we have are found in the Book of Job; Job says that the throne of God lays on the side of the north. You see, according to Revelation 20:10 and 11, dirt, grass, cities, the earth, the heavens, the stars, and "the universe" are no longer in existence at the time of the judgment.

Rather than taking place upon a specific, physical locale, Judgment Day takes place in the presence of God. Judgment does not take place in a hall, a courtroom, an arena, or a coliseum; it is not even on a battlefield like Armageddon. In fact, there is nothing to stand on because there is nothing left. This is a fulfillment of prophecy found in 2 Peter 3:10, a passage of scripture that says, "But the day of the Lord will come as a thief in the night; in the which the heavens shall pass away with a great noise, and the elements shall melt with fervent heat, the earth also and the works that are therein shall be burned up." In other words, a day is coming in which the heavens and the earth shall be dissolved by fire.

The Bible speaks of a word called regeneration, which means "to take something and to make it new." In Biblical terms this means to make something born again. The Bible only speaks of regeneration in two places in the New Testament: Titus 3:5 and Matthew 19. Paul tells us in Titus, "Not by works of righteousness which we have done, but according to his mercy he saved us, by the washing of regeneration, and renewing of the Holy Ghost." We are made born again, not because of what we are able to do but who He is. Matthew 19 teaches us that the earth and the heavens will

> *Judgment Day takes place standing face to face in the presence of God.*

one day be regenerated. So, remember this: when Judgment Day takes place, all that you and I know as the physical world is no longer in existence.

109

Keep in mind, however, that the events found in Revelation chapter 21 are coming! There is going to be a new Heaven! There is going to be a new earth! There is going to be a New Jerusalem! Judgment Day takes place in His Presence, not necessarily in a specific place. Humanity is famous for spending time, money and resources trying to run from God, but we cannot hide from His presence! You see, Judgment Day takes place standing face to face in the presence of God.

WHY IS JUDGMENT DAY SO IMPORTANT?

That leads to an interesting follow-up question. Why is Judgment Day so important? Those who have rejected Jesus Christ have already been condemned. Are they not already residing within the lake of fire? Are they not already within hell? Do they not already have their leader, Satan, with them? Why would God bring them up and finally sentence them in His presence to an eternity known as the lake of fire? I think this is something our culture and even our churches so desperately need to hear. Why does Judgment Day take place? Judgment Day takes place because of the seriousness of sin. Sin is not a result of your culture; sin is not a result of your upbringing. Sin is not a result of your background or your personality. Sin is rebellion against God.

Revelation 21:8 says, "But the fearful, and unbelieving, and the abominable, and murderers, and whoremongers, and sorcerers, and idolaters." Those words make my skin crawl. The Bible says those people shall not inherit the Kingdom of God. The fearful, unbelieving, abominable and such will not enter into the new Heaven, the new earth, and the New Jerusalem. Those who are not found written in the book of life will not be allowed to live in the presence of God.

Notice the last description of people: "and all liars." Every human being has rebelled against God. Every human being lives a life of lies and rebellion against God. If you don't believe me, volunteer and serve in the preschool. If you have not had a two or a three year old in your home lately, let me remind you of this: they are all liars - and so are we. Ask a two year old, "Did you color on the wall?" With crayon in-hand the two year old says, "Nope." And we do this as adults as well.

You see, we do not take sin seriously any more. We chalk it up to things like the culture, environment, or personality. According to Revelation

21:8 any time we go against the things of God our sin is so serious that it deserves "burning with fire and brimstone: which is the second death." Judgment Day does not occur because God wants to finally, once and for all, prove He is God. It is not some big show where He says, "Aha! Let me go ahead and do some big grand finale." Sentencing takes place because sin is serious.

HOW DOES JUDGMENT DAY OCCUR?
That leads me to my final question: how does Judgment Day occur? How does it take place? We know those who have rejected Jesus are ultimately sentenced. We know judgment happens between Gog and Magog and the new Heaven and the new earth. We know judgment is in the presence of God and we know it is because of the seriousness of our sin. But, this may be the most important question that we ask: How does judgment occur? And the answer is this: in absolute silence. 111

I have had the privilege of debating and discussing the truths of God's Word and the validity of the exclusivity of Jesus Christ—that He is the only way—with hundreds, if not thousands of people. I have discussed these truths with atheists, pagans, heathens, and non-believing Baptists. Everyone who wants to go against the truth of Jesus Christ always has an argument. They always have a philosophy, they always have a point of debate and it goes something like this: "Well, in my opinion," or "I've read," "I've heard," "My perspective," "According to so-and-so." Revelation 20 says that the books were opened and those that were dead were judged according to their works. You will notice that no one raises their hand in objection. No one says, "But I've got a good point." When you stand in the presence of Almighty God and you have seen the heavens and the earth dissolve away, you realize that whatever you thought was a good argument is not worth anything. You understand that whatever you thought was a good perspective, an incredible philosophy, or an educated hypothesis looks ignorant in His presence.

Philippians 2:10-11 is a passage of scripture regarding Judgment Day: "That at the name of Jesus every knee should bow, of things in heaven, and things in earth, and things under the earth; And that every tongue should confess that Jesus Christ is Lord, to the glory of God the Father."

You may have an argument, you may have a debate, you may be able to discuss your opinions or you may have a philosophy for why you do not believe in God. You may have someone who claimed to be a believer that is a hypocrite and you use their actions as an excuse to reject Christ. You can have an argument, or excuse or anything you want, but understand this truth: the Bible says one day every one of us will confess that Jesus is Lord. Every one of us will bow our knee. The question is not *if* you are going to bow; the question is after you bow where will you spend eternity? Those who have confessed their sin, received forgiveness and professed faith in Christ during their lives will go to everlasting life—the new Heaven, the new earth, the New Jerusalem. But those who do not have faith in Christ will experience the second death.

Everything in Revelation builds to the fact that one day every one of us will give an account to God as to whether we have believed and received Christ or we have rejected the truth of Jesus. There are those of you who have had excuses. You have had your positions and your

112

philosophies. According to the Word of God you are going to kneel, you are going to bow, and you are going to confess Jesus Christ as Lord one day, and you want to do it on this side of breathing your last breath, not on the other side. In fact, when the Bible says that every knee will bow that means the devil's knees, the demons' knees, the principalities' knees, the philosophers' knees, the academicians' knees, the rebellious' knees, that means everybody's knees—even the "good" people who were good in the eyes of man but rejected the truth of Jesus Christ—they will bow their knees to Christ! If you have not bowed your knee, if you have never confessed Jesus as Lord, consider making a confession of sin today and placing your faith in Jesus Christ.

Chapter 7

The New Heaven, Earth, and Jerusalem

What has humanity dreamed of since its creation? No pain. No misery. No disappointment. No frustrations. No temptations. No sorrow. No heartache. No destruction. No struggles. No tears. No sickness. No death. No darkness. The dream has now become a reality. It sounds like fiction. It sounds like a figment of one's imagination. But this is not fiction, this is fact built upon faith. It is a life like none other. It is . . . the New Heaven, Earth, and Jerusalem.

If you remember from the introduction of this book, I have organized this study of Revelation in a similar fashion to the *Star Wars* saga written by George Lucas. In the saga's final story, story number six which was the third movie, there is celebration, there is a rejoicing that darkness has been defeated, that light has won, that the characters everyone was excited about ended up being victorious and the ones we all wanted to "boo" ended up in demise. And yet, it wasn't actually the last movie. It was the sixth and final story, but it was the middle movie.

One of the things we desire to do in studying the Book of Revelation is to have a greater understanding of the concepts such as the great tribulation, the character of the Antichrist, judgment day, the millennium, and Armageddon. At this point in our study we come to that final issue, that final subject matter that is addressed in the book of Revelation: the fact that there is a New Heaven, a New Earth and a New Jerusalem. The reason that I wanted to address the New Heaven in the middle of the study is because at this point (the end of the actual Book of Revelation, but the midpoint of our study) I want to have everything fully developed. I want you to know how it is all going to end, to know about all the characters so that you can begin focusing on the very exciting things at the beginning of the Book of Revelation. And I also want you to prepare yourself to respond to the truths that you have learned in the Book of Revelation.

Before we turn to Revelation chapters 21 and 22 let me share with you that this is the great culmination. This is everything that we sing about. This is everything that the church of Jesus Christ stands for. If you have understood that you are a sinner, needing a Savior, have asked Jesus to forgive you of your sins and save you then you are what the Bible calls born again. You have thought thoughts, you have dreamed dreams, you have heard sermons, and you have sung songs about the New Heaven. Scriptures tell us that no mind has any idea of how great Heaven is going to be. This is why the apostles came to Jesus in John 14 and He made the statement, "In my Father's house are many mansions: if it were not so, I would have told you. I go to prepare a place for you. And if I go and prepare a place for you, I will come again, and receive you unto myself; that where I am, there you may be also." This is everything that the Christian faith is leading us toward. When we put our lives in the hands of Jesus Christ, we are promised an amazing eternity.

118   Revelation chapter 21, verse 1 through chapter 22, verse 5 is about the New Heaven, New Earth and New Jerusalem. Revelation chapter 22:6 onward actually explains how we are to respond to this information. Revelation 21:1-7 says:

> And I saw a new heaven and a new earth: for the first heaven and the first earth were passed away; and there was no more sea. And I John saw the holy city, new Jerusalem, coming down from God out of heaven, prepared as a bride adorned for her husband. And I heard a great voice out of heaven saying, Behold, the tabernacle of God is with men, and he will dwell with them, and they shall be his people, and God himself shall be with them, and be their God. And God shall wipe away all tears from their eyes; and there shall be no more death, neither sorrow, nor crying, neither shall there be any more pain: for the former things are passed away. And

he that sat upon the throne said, Behold, I make all things new. And he said unto me, Write: for these words are true and faithful. And he said unto me, It is done. I am Alpha and Omega, the beginning and the end. I will give unto him that is athirst of the fountain of the water of life freely. He that overcometh shall inherit all things; and I will be his God, and he shall be my son."

This passage about the New Heaven, the New Earth and the New Jerusalem in simplistic terms, describes eternity for the believer in Jesus Christ. For the rejecter of Jesus Christ, for the one who says, "I would rather live life my own way and not God's way," their end is described in chapter 20 with the final judgment, the lake of fire, and the second death. But for those who have humbled themselves before the cross, confessed they need a Savior named Jesus, their future is the New 119 Heaven and the New Earth.

HOW DO WE KNOW HEAVEN IS REAL?

The first question is very critical. How do we know Heaven is even true? Be honest, does this not seem like "Biblical pie in the sky?" All former things are passed away; there is no more crying, there are no more tears, there is no more darkness. This is everything we have hoped for but none of us has ever experienced it. There might be those who say, "This just sounds too good to be true." So, how do we know it's true?

The first reason we know it is true is because John had a vision. Now understand, if humanity does something so they can see the ethereal, so they can see God, we call that a hallucination. A vision is when God opens up the heavens, He parts the heavens and says, "Son, I need you to see this." There are several very famous visions in scripture. One of the most famous is in Isaiah chapter 6 where the prophet, Isaiah, said he saw the Lord high and lifted up. He saw the train of His robe filling the pillars of Heaven. God had the seraphim come and put the stone upon Isaiah's lips because He knew he was an unclean man. Isaiah actually saw God face to face; he saw the heavens open up. A couple of books later we have a prophet by the name of Ezekiel. In Ezekiel chapter 1 it says that he was looking toward the north and out of the clouds came the throne of God. It talks about all of these wheels within a wheel and that the throne came and went as it chose. There were cherubim at its base.

For a more practical perspective we look to the book of Acts chapter 10 and there we find a man by the name of Peter, one of the early

120 apostles. He was praying one day on top of a roof and the Bible says he had a vision; there was a sheet that was lowered with every form of animal, both "clean and unclean." The Lord told Peter never to call unclean that which He declared clean; rise and eat. Then we have the Book of Revelation chapter 21 where the Apostle John says in verse 1, "I saw," verse 2, "I saw," verse 3, "I heard." On and on through chapters 21 and 22 he says "I saw," and "I heard."

Now I do not know about you, but I have known a lot of people who claim they have seen a lot of things and they claim they have heard a lot of voices. So how do we know that this vision is something upon which we can literally stake our eternity? John's vision was not just a hallucination, or something man wanted to see. His vision is from God and is validated by scripture. Notice what the Bible says at the end of Revelation verse 5, "Write: for these words are true and faithful." Visions are verified by scripture.

Notice the order in which God gave the prophets visions. God gave scripture well in advance of visions so that when prophets saw the scripture fulfilled they knew the visions were from God. For example, when Isaiah said I have seen the Lord high and lifted up he is experiencing what was already explained by the Psalmist. You see, three hundred years before Isaiah's vision the Lord inspired the Psalmist to describe Him as holy, and as One whose robe filled the temple. Then, three hundred years later Isaiah actually saw God's holiness displayed; he saw Him high and lifted up! When Ezekiel said I look to the north and out of a whirlwind I saw the throne of God, literally hundreds of years earlier a man by the name of Job wrote the same message. When the apostle, Peter, declared that no one was outside 121 of the grace of God, no one would be shielded from the saving message but all clean and unclean could be saved he was reiterating a message that was written down in Genesis chapters 12 through 15 when God came to Abraham and said, "I have made you a messenger to all nations." Likewise, John's vision in Revelation 21 and 22 was a representation of what Isaiah wrote about a thousand years earlier when he penned Isaiah 65 and 66 describing the New Jerusalem, New Heaven and New Earth.

The New Jerusalem is not true because we want it to be true. It is not true because John saw a vision. It is true because the Lord wrote it down, John saw the vision, and the vision verified what God had already said. The word was not written after the fact; the word preceded the vision.

THE REPLACEMENT AND RENEWAL OF ITEMS IN NEW JERUSALEM

John saw two main items: the replacement and the renewal of *items*, and the replacement and the renewal of *issues*. This passage is most commonly known as describing the New Heaven, New Earth and New Jerusalem. Interestingly enough, in Revelation 21 there is not much mention of the New Earth or the New Heaven. However, there is quite a bit about the "New Jerusalem," that heavenly city prepared as a bride that will descend out of Heaven to the earth and where the bride of Christ, those who have believed on Him as their Savior, shall dwell for all of eternity.

A Picture of New Jerusalem

Revelation 21: 14-16 actually gives some interesting measurements:

And the wall of the city had twelve foundations, and in them the names of the twelve apostles of the Lamb. And he that talked with me had a golden reed to measure the city, and the gates thereof, and the wall thereof. And the city lieth foursquare, and the length is as large as the breadth: and he measured the city with the reed, twelve thousand furlongs. The length and the breadth and the height of it are equal.

We could postulate a lot about what the New Earth is going to look like and what the New Heaven is going to look like, but because we are told, at least in brief, what New Jerusalem will look like, I want to place our focus there. The Word of God tells us that the length, width and height of New Jerusalem have the same measurement. The city is three dimensional instead of two dimensional. Some people believe the city could easily be a cube that measures twelve thousand furlongs in length. A furlong is typically about 582 feet. Twelve thousand furlongs equates to roughly 1,320 miles. Most Bible commentators say that the length of the city is anywhere between 1,200 and 1,500 miles.

To place this in perspective, imagine driving from Washington, D.C. down to Miami, Florida; go west to Dallas, Texas; north to Chicago and then back east to Washington, D.C. In essence, you have driven a route in the shape of a square. The route from Washington D.C. to Miami, Florida is roughly 1500 miles, and so it goes from city to city. The perimeter you have driven roughly equals the perimeter of the New Jerusalem. Now imagine going up about 1500 miles. Because the New Jerusalem measures about 1500 miles in length, width and height it is possible that the city forms the shape of a cube. That is about the perimeter of this length. Now imagine going up the same distance. It measures that distance in all areas so many say it must be in the shape or the form of a cube. There is nothing wrong with that idea. In fact, the Bible says that the width, length and height are the same.

We can agree on this—the city is going to be big! And it will be a city like none other.

There are others who would say the shape is not really a cube but a pyramidal shape. Isaiah 28:16 prophesied that Jesus Christ was the cornerstone. The stone that is rejected is the cornerstone, the One that establishes the foundation of New Jerusalem. First Peter 2:6 says the stone that was rejected, this same cornerstone is Jesus Christ. Psalm 118:22 says the same cornerstone is made the head of the corner. There are those that believe New Jerusalem is a pyramidal shape building where the head is actually the cornerstone. Allow me to

123

share with you my honest opinion: The city might be in the form of a cube or it might be in the form of a pyramid, but I do not think we are going to care! We can agree on this—the city is going to be big! And it will be a city like none other.

The Parameters of New Jerusalem

Most of us understand dimension such as length and width, but sometimes it is hard to conceptualize height. Do you realize that you can board an airplane and fly at forty thousand feet above the ground and you will still be more than a thousand miles shy of the height of New Jerusalem? How big is that? Well, if you consider that the city is in the form of a cube, then those dimensions make the city about two billion cubic miles. "Cubic" is the key word there, not two billion square miles but two billion cubic miles. Understand this, the New Jerusalem is the picture of either a cube or a pyramid, and its parameters of two billion cubic miles are almost infinite in our finite minds! (By the way, if you believe the city is a pyramid, then the city is only a mere five hundred million cubic miles!) In other words, the New Jerusalem is not a little, small place! Its enormity is more than our finite minds can comprehend. There is more room in the New Jerusalem than you have ever owned. There is more room than you could have ever dreamed!

The People of New Jerusalem

What about the people? After all, Revelation 21:8 tells us of those who will not enter the city. The Bible says that only those who have been covered by the blood of Jesus Christ, those who are written in the Book of Life, will enter the New Jerusalem. So, how many people will

124

actually reside in New Jerusalem? Let me share with you four of my favorite words when studying the Book of Revelation: I do not know! However, there are those who are smarter than me who claim to know how many people have been on planet earth. A very secular, very academic, non-Biblical perspective, full-blown Darwinian evolution perspective claims that there have been about one hundred billion people on this planet. A conservative Biblical perspective claims that about twenty billion people have lived on earth.

Consider that one hundred billion people have been on earth since Adam and Eve. In Matthew 7 Jesus said broad is the road to destruction, narrow is the way of righteousness. Because the road to destruction is broad, I am going to consider that at least 51 percent of all of humanity will not be in the New Jerusalem. That would leave us with about 50 billion people. Some of you may be wondering how big your mansion in Heaven will be. Well, considering that there needs to be enough room to accommodate 50 billion people, and using the parameters of a pyramid structure rather than a cube (keeping in mind that the pyramid is the smaller parameter), then your measly, little apartment in the New Jerusalem would have a floor plan of 25,000 square feet over 50 stories high! Are you upset about that? And made of gold that can be seen through! When we talk about New Jerusalem it is literally a structure we cannot fathom! We cannot imagine it in its fullness! And that is exciting!

THE REPLACEMENT AND RENEWAL OF ISSUES OF LIFE IN NEW JERUSALEM

I think the most important thing that John saw in his vision is the renewal or the replacement of the issues of life. Revelation 21:4 says,

"And God shall wipe away all tears from their eyes; and there shall be no more death, neither sorrow, nor crying, neither shall there be any more pain: for the former things are passed away." In Heaven death is eliminated, sorrow is eliminated, and crying has been replaced with celebration. Understand this, for the believer in Christ death has been replaced by a very distinct life. Revelation 21:27 says, "And there shall in no wise enter into it any thing that defiles, neither whatsoever worketh abomination, or makes a lie: but they which are written in the Lamb's book of life."

On this planet you and I know the sting of untimely death. We experience the death of our physical bodies, the death of dreams, the death of relationships, and the death of hopes. But the Bible tells us that in the New Jerusalem there is no more abomination and no more death! You see, in Heaven a life without death replaces death itself!

126

There is something else that has been replaced or renewed in New Jerusalem: a life of sunshine instead of sorrow. Revelation 21:23 says, "And the city had no need of the sun, neither of the moon, to shine in it: for the glory of God did light it, and the Lamb is the light thereof." Our lives in Heaven consist of an existence without sorrow, without depression, without frustration, without angst, without anger, without the blues or without darkness! There is no darkness; there is no sun, but there is always light—a light that comes from God and it is the only Son-shine we will need.

Do you ever wonder what are we going to do in Heaven for all of eternity? Are we going to sit on the clouds with the angels and play harps? As a very non-musical individual, that does not sound like

Heaven to me. So, what will it be like? Revelation 21:24 says, "And the nations of them which are saved shall walk in the light of it: and the kings of the earth do bring their glory and honor into it."

I have never attended a royal parade, but I have seen one on television. If there is anybody who can throw a celebration it is royalty; it is kings and queens. They can throw a party like none other. Revelation 21:24 does not mention just one single king or a queen; it says, "... the kings of the earth bring their glory and honor into it." Our world is so entrapped by crying, tears and disappointments that it is hard to imagine a consistent time of celebration where there will be no death, no sorrow, no crying! But, Heaven will be a time when all of our heartache and disappointment will be replaced with celebration. In other words, we will be attending a party to top all parties. You have been invited to this party, so why would you not want to attend?

127

It gets better! Not only do we experience no death, no sorrow or no crying, there is no more pain! Pain has been replaced by prosperity. Revelation 22:3 says, "There shall be no more curse." Genesis 3 gives the account of Adam and Eve's fall into sin. The curse of that sin brought death. But in the New Jerusalem death does not exist; it is no longer there! The curse of sin brought sorrow, but in the New Jerusalem sorrow is gone. The curse of sin brought misery, anguish, and crying, but in the New Jerusalem those things will exist no more. The curse brought toilsome, painful, hard work, but in the New Jerusalem there is no more pain! The curse will be lifted, and our pain will be gone!

Allow me, for a brief moment, to address a twenty-first century Christianity issue that brings me much concern. One of the greatest "enemies" to Biblical Christianity is not atheism, paganism or voodoo.

Instead, I believe the "prosperity gospel" is harming us in grave proportions. In fact, the prosperity gospel is propagating the air waves; it is propagating the world. It teaches the idea that "Christians are the tail and they get to wag God and have Him do anything they want, provide anything they want, at any time they want." Without sounding too harsh, I believe such teaching is heresy. Heresy literally means "erroneous teaching." Let me give you the "Jeff Meyers'" definition of heresy: the right teaching at the wrong time. The problem with the prosperity gospel is this: it teaches that the curse has *already* been lifted. However, each day I experience sorrow, crying and some pain, either in my own life or I see it in the lives of others and you do, too. People, understand this: the curse has not been lifted yet. Last time I checked, work is still hard. Weeds still grow in my yard! People still experience sorrow! People still experience death! People still cry, and people still have pain! Why? Because we live in a cursed world, it is a cursed life.

128

But the Bible says one day the curse will be lifted! You see, the prosperity gospel is true not *now*, but in the *future*—when we enter the New Heaven, the New Earth and the New Jerusalem. In that place anything we need and want will be there. There will be no painful toiling, no anguish, and no sorrow. All those issues of life are one day replaced; not on *this* side of life, but on *that* side of eternity.

OUR RESPONSE TO THE NEW JERUSALEM

So, how do we respond to all this information about the New Jerusalem? How does the reality of a New Heaven change how we live today? How does it affect how we live tomorrow? Revelation 22:6 gives us an every day, practical "how-do-we-respond" answer.

In fact, it shows us how to respond in two areas: on the inside and on the outside.

An Inside Response

How do I respond on the inside? Revelation 22:9 says, "Then he said unto me, See thou do it not: for I am thy fellow servant (the Apostle John had fallen down at the angel's feet to worship him) and of thy brethren the prophets, and of them which keep the saying of this book: worship God." Our study of the Book of Revelation, our knowledge of the New Heaven, the New Earth, and the New Jerusalem ought to make us more excited about worshipping God than we have ever been in all of our lives. The truth of our future should make us excited on the inside, and because we know what He has prepared for us, we should bring Him worship and praise! When Jesus said I have 129 a mansion prepared for you, He was not lying. In fact, it is actually bigger than you and I could ever imagine. We ought to fall prostrate before God and worship Him. We should worship God not just on Sunday but on every day. Worship ought to be the primary focus of our lives. Knowing all that awaits us in heaven should change how we worship the One true God.

It should also change how we pray. Revelation 22:20 says, "Come quickly, Lord Jesus." In other words, the trappings of this world should fade away, the things that so entice us should become dismal. Our prayer lives ought to be more concerned about eternity and who is going to be there than our little hangnail that is bothering us. The reality of a New Heaven ought to change our prayer lives in such a way that we become more concerned about praying for our neighbors, for those in our community, for those on the other side of the planet, and for those who have never heard the gospel of Jesus Christ. When we grasp the message found in Revelation chapters 21 and 22, it should make us worship God with an endearing passion and it should change our prayer lives.

An Outside Response

A heavenly view should also change us on the outside because what we ought to do is take the message and share it! Like Jesus says: you should not take the candle and put it under a bushel, you should proclaim it. Revelation 22:10 says, "And he said unto me, Seal not the sayings of the prophecy of this book: for the time is at hand." In the book of Daniel, God came to the prophet, Daniel, and said I

130 am going to give you something but do not tell them. In Revelation, chapter 10 He comes to the Apostle John and says I am going to give you a message; eat it, drink it, take it but do not tell them. When we get to Revelation 22 everything changes. All that John saw and learned was to be told. Everything he understood about the tribulation, the Antichrist, judgment day, the millennium, the New Heaven was to be shared! God was saying, "Do not keep it sealed. Do not keep your mouth shut. Talk about it, share it and let people know." Our understanding of the things we have learned from God through Revelation ought to change us on the outside because now we know how the story ends. We know who wins, and we know what the New Jerusalem looks like.

Revelation 22:18 says, "For I testify unto every man that hears the words of the prophecy of this book, If any man shall add unto these things, God shall add unto him the plagues that are written in this book." We have studied subject matters that are controversial even within the church, much less outside of the church. I will testify that when you begin to propagate, promote and proclaim the truth of the great tribulation, the person of the Antichrist, the final judgment and the reality that those who reject Jesus will spend forever in an eternity called hell and the lake of fire, it is real easy to skip over some of the harsh truth. I am reminded of Luke 12:48 where Jesus said this state-ment, "To whomever much is given, much is required." Our knowledge of the truths found in Revelation should encourage us to proclaim the message, but we need also to preserve the message and not water down the truth found within the book.

> *He is going to reign forever and ever and ever—and do not ever let anyone talk you out of it!*

I want to give you a charge from the bottom of my heart. I have been in the 131 classrooms, in the midst of the debates and at the kitchen tables with skeptical people, and I have heard what learned men and women think are logical arguments against the gospel. My challenge is this: Do not let anyone talk you out of proclaiming and preserving the message of Jesus Christ. Do not let any theologian, pastor, television preacher or wacko out there convince you that what you have read will not come to pass and is not true. Do not fall for it. You ask, "What if I do fall for a lie?" Listen to what Revelation 22 says: the plagues will be added unto you. I am not a rocket scientist, but I am at least smart enough to know that I am not interested in experiencing plagues. I have read about locusts and hail the size of basketballs. I do not want to experience any part of that kind of plague.

Titus 2 says look unto His blessed coming. The end of the Book of Revelation says there is a place that you could never imagine. In fact, you could not paint it; you cannot imagine how incredible it is. If you will live for Christ and anticipate the reality of the New Jerusalem, then the Lord will do exactly what the third verse of chapter one says: He will bless you! Do not let anyone—no matter who he is, what he says or what his credentials are—talk you out of the truth that is contained therein. Jesus Christ did not *just* come through a virgin birth, He did not *just* come and live a sinless life, He did not *just* die on a cross, He did not *just* arise from the dead, He did not *just* ascend on high, He is not just going to return one day, He is not *just* going to win at the Battle of Armageddon, He is not *just* going to sit on a throne for a thousand years in Jerusalem, He *is* going to reign forever and ever and ever—and do not ever let anyone talk you out of it!

Chapter 8

Prediction or Prophecy

On the island of Patmos a first century Roman dictator has isolated a pastor by the name of John. It appears that no one will hear him or his message again. Then a voice sounds and a figure appears. It is not a Roman but Jesus Christ. He informs John that the future of the Universe is at stake. John has been selected to write what he sees. The vision is to be published throughout the world. Is it a prediction or is it a prophecy?

Have you ever wondered if the Book of Revelation is merely a prediction or is it truly a prophecy? How we answer that question determines how your life and my life are altered and changed. Revelation 1:1-3 introduces us to the content of the Book of Revelation and provides us with an answer to the prediction or prophecy question.

Revelation 1:1-3 says, "The Revelation of Jesus Christ, which God gave unto him, to show unto his servants things which must shortly come to pass; and he sent and signified it by his angel unto his servant John: Who bare record of the word of God, and of the testimony of Jesus Christ, and of all things that he saw. Blessed is he that readeth, and they that hear the words of this prophecy, and keep those things which are written therein: for the time is at hand."

What is Revelation? Ask the question, and instead of relying on someone else's answer, look to the testimony of the Book of Revelation for your answer.

If there was a theme throughout the Book of Revelation, it would be the last statement in verse 3, "for the time is at hand." The Book of Revelation has so many unique concepts, issues and characters; it is a book of great wonder, but it also provides great purpose for our lives. Which brings us to some very important questions: what is the purpose of Revelation, why was it written and why was it given to us?

Have you noticed that every time you open a book on the subject of Revelation that it contradicts or conflicts with another book you have

135

already read? We usually fall on two cliffs. Either we have read so much that we have what I call a "cafeteria faith:" a little bit from here and a little from there and when you put it all together it becomes a casserole of theology that tastes the same. Or, we tend to stray so far away from the content of the book of Revelation that we will not even read it all. So whatever your position, will you allow today to be the day that you look at this incredible book of the Bible with fresh eyes? Can we take a step back from the commentaries you have read or the books you have read and can we simply ask this question: What is Revelation? Ask the question, and instead of relying on someone else's answer, look to the testimony of the Book of Revelation for your answer.

WHO IS THE PRIMARY CHARACTER IN THE BOOK OF REVELATION?

The first question we have to ask is this: Who is the primary character in the book of Revelation? This is not a trick question; the answer is as simple as it sounds. A multitude of characters are revealed throughout the book. After all, in Revelation 1:9-10 we are introduced to a man by the name of John, who is living on the island of Patmos during the first century. He is "in the Spirit" on the Lord's Day. The Lord comes to John in a way that he has never seen Him and gives John a vision. The Apostle John—the same John whom the Bible calls the beloved apostle, the same John who leaned against Jesus as they ate their meals, the same apostle through whom God gave us the Gospel of John and the letters of I, II and III John—this same man is seen throughout much of the Book of Revelation, yet he is not the primary character. We are also introduced to an individual known as the Antichrist. Revelation also reveals to us the two witnesses of God. Another character is an angel who so vividly represents the person of God that John catches himself worshipping him, only to be reminded by the angel that wor-

136

ship is reserved for Jesus Christ alone.

You see, within the Book of Revelation there is a myriad of characters; however, there is only one central character in the Book of Revelation and that character is revealed in the first five words of the book. Understand this: the revelation is not focused on the person of John, nor is it an attempt to magnify the character of the Antichrist. From the very beginning of the Book of Revelation we read these words, "The Revelation of Jesus Christ." As you study the Book of Revelation, if you somehow take your focus off of the person Jesus Christ, then you have derailed—gotten off-track, so-to-speak. If you dive into everything else the book describes instead of focusing on Jesus, then you have missed the message. Without a doubt, the purpose of this book, the last book of the Bible, is to show us the person of Jesus Christ.

> *Without a doubt, the purpose of this book, the last book of the Bible, is to show us the person of Jesus Christ.*

137

Consider the previous topics that we have studied throughout the chapters of the book you hold in your hand. From Revelation 11:15 we learned that the kingdoms of the world are transferred from one person to another. Do you remember to whom the kingdoms are transferred? They are transferred to the person of Jesus Christ. When we studied what we know as the great tribulation—that time period the Book of Daniel calls Daniel's Seventieth Week, the one that is also prophesied as Jacob's trouble, that time period that Jesus alluded to in Matthew 24 and 25, that seven year time period that is horrific on earth—do you remember how it begins? The great tribulation begins with Jesus Christ and a book sealed with seven seals.

In Revelation chapter 5 this book is presented from the throne of God. No one above earth, no one on earth, no one under earth is able to open the contents, but then Someone shows up! That Someone is described as being of the Tribe of Judah, and He looked as if He was a Lamb that was slain. That Someone is Jesus Christ! He opens up the seven seals, and a rider on a horse appears—a man whom we know as the Antichrist. It is interesting that the mere name, Antichrist, shows a complete contradiction to the person of Jesus Christ. You see, everything about the Antichrist—his actions, his words, even his name—goes against the person of Jesus Christ. Yet, interestingly enough, even the enemy of Christ, the Antichrist and all of his actions, highlights the magnificence of Jesus Christ. The opposition only bolsters the character and significance of Christ. You see, all throughout the Book of Revelation the focus is upon the Savior, Jesus Christ. He alone is the Great Character.

To support this concept even further, take a look at Armageddon. Who splits the skies? Who comes on a white horse? Who has a sword coming out of His mouth and feet as brass? Who destroys His enemies? The person of Jesus Christ! Revelation 20 describes a throne that is placed in Jerusalem, and for a thousand years Satan is bound and Someone else reigns on high. Who is the reigning King? Jesus Christ. At the final judgment, all of the nations, all people, are gathered—both the dead, small and great, rich and poor—and to Whom are they accountable? They stand accountable for eternity to Jesus Christ. Who speaks the New Heaven, the New Earth, and the New Jerusalem into creation? Once again, Jesus Christ!

You see, whether you are studying the millennium, Armageddon, or the Antichrist you cannot remove the person of Jesus Christ. If you steer off of Jesus then you have missed the message of Revelation. If you get off of Jesus then you have gotten off-track. If you, or anyone else, spend so much time nit-picking chronology, details, and expectations and there is no mention of the person of Jesus Christ, then you miss the whole message of the Book of Revelation. The Book of Revelation is about the person of Jesus Christ.

WHAT IS THE BOOK OF REVELATION?
The Book of Revelation is either a prediction or prophecy. A prediction is when someone draws a specific conclusion based from a certain set of knowledge, facts or pieces of information. A prophecy is information that is beyond foresight, beyond one's control. In fact a prophecy is of such magnitude that often a prophet of the Lord 139 cannot even imagine how the prophecy could come to fruition. Also, a prophecy from the Lord involves an elapsed time period. In other words, the time period between the spoken prophecy and its fruition is so great that the prophet could not possibly have a hand in seeing such a prophecy fulfilled.

A prediction is when one makes a claim based on a certain set of variables, a certain set of numbers, and a certain set of facts. We laugh in our society about the meteorologists and the weathermen because they have all the radars you can put money into and they get the weather right one time out of ten, but they still get a raise the next year! Isn't it incredible how that works! You see, they are making predictions based on a low pressure system, a particular cold front, etc. They formulate a prediction from the knowledge at hand.

The Difference Between Prediction and Prophecy

Let's try to experience the difference between a prediction and a prophecy. Pick a number. For the sake of this illustration, you might want to choose a small number unless you have a degree in mathematics. Choose a small number, but if you have a calculator with you or a pen and paper then feel free to pick a big number. (By the way, do not get creative; the number has to be a positive number, so don't pick negative three!) Once you have that number in mind, I want you to add seven to it. So if you picked the number 10, you now have 17. After you add seven, take the new number and multiply it by two. After you have multiplied by two, take the new number and subtract four. After you have subtracted four then divide by two. Now subtract the original number. (Now you see why I told you to pick a small number!) If you followed my directions and you added, multiplied, divided and sub-

> The message of Revelation is built on three things: the Word of God, a future element, and a fulfillment of the prophecy.

140

tracted correctly, I am going to make this prediction: The number you ended up with is the number five. How did I know that? Well, I knew the conclusion before I began. (And for those of you who are shaking your head strangely, you do end up with five if you do it right!) If you chose the number 10, the mathematics would look like this: 10+7=17, 17x2=34, 34-4=30, 30/2=15, 15-10=5 You see, a prediction is something that anyone in any field with any amount of knowledge in any situation can somewhat do.

A prophecy, on the other side of the equation, is what Revelation 1:2 refers to when it says that John "bore the record of the Word of God, the testimony of Jesus and all the things that he saw." The message of Revelation is built on three things: the Word of God, a future element, and a fulfillment of the prophecy.

Prophecy is Based on the Word of God

First, the message has as its foundation the Word of God. There are 404 verses in the Book of Revelation. There are over 200 quotations or illustrations from the Old Testament. In other words, this is not new information. Through the person of John the Lord Himself is giving a clearer picture of the messages of Isaiah, the messages of Ezekiel, and the messages of Daniel. Notice the order of events. The first thing mentioned in Revelation 1:2 is that the message given to John is the 141 Word of God. The last thing given to John is the vision, the things that he saw. So if a man, a woman, a book, a TV evangelist claims to see something that does not match up with the Word of God, please quit sending them money! The Word of God is the foundation for prophecy. Prophecy is not just an idea or a claim made by a particular person. Prophecy is based on and has its foundation on the Word of God.

Prophecy Contains a Future Element

The second aspect of prophecy is this: it must contain a significant element regarding the future. Now when I say the future, I really mean the future. Revelation 1:2 says the "testimony of Jesus Christ." An example of this "testimony" is seen in Revelation 19, the famous Armageddon passage, when Jesus physically comes to earth. You see, the Bible says the spirit of prophecy is the testimony of Jesus Christ. That means there must be a significant time period when the principle person writing the prophecy is removed in order for the message to be a prophecy and not a prediction.

Allow me to use another weather illustration. In recent days, the state of Alabama was overcome with devastating tornadoes. About twenty minutes before the tragedies occurred, learned men and women all over the country sent out warning signals. Based on the weather and based on the barometric pressure, they predicted that something awful was about to happen. They did not provide a prophecy, they spoke a prediction. Imagine, however, making the following statement: In 586 years in a town that has never been developed, in a country that does not exist, a person who has not been born will be the true Messiah. That is prophecy. Revelation 1:2 says, "…the testimony of Jesus." You see, the last prophecy about Jesus Christ was written 400 years before He was ever born of a virgin.

142

Prophecy Comes to Fruition

The foundation for prophecy is scripture. The future is a key element. And, one of the key aspects of prophecy is that it comes to fruition, or it comes to pass. I think this is where most people get so off-base when studying the Book of Revelation. They watch the news, they read the newspapers, they have a conversation, they observe something with their eyes, and based on what they see and hear they determine that all this "could be the sixth seal." They are not speaking words of prophecy they are guessing or making a prediction.

Do you realize there were 48 specific prophecies about the life, death and resurrection of Jesus in the Old Testament? All of them were written at least 400 years before Jesus was ever born of a virgin. Do you know that the statistical probability of all those things occurring in the life of one man exactly as they were prophesied is one times ten to the one hundred fifty-seventh? That is a 1 with a lot of zeroes behind it! Do you realize that number is even larger than the number of electrons in the known universe? Forty-eight prophecies! Micah 5:2 says that Jesus would be born in Bethlehem. Was He born in a suburb? Was this baby born of Mary? The Bible says that His enemies would gamble for His clothes, and they did!

We do not have to play a guessing game with the truths of the Bible. When the Bible says that the moon goes red, the moon goes red. When it says the sun goes black, the sun goes black. When it says the waters are turned to blood, they do not just turn red from an oil-spill; they become blood. We do not have to guess. We do not have to speculate because every prophecy about the life of Jesus, the death of Jesus and the resurrection of Jesus happened exactly as it was spoken hundreds of years ago. Hundreds of years ago the Lord told us what is going to happen and what He said will come to fruition. The Apostle John could have nothing to do with what is going to happen because he no longer lives here on earth. There is no way he could have known the world that we live in today and the way in which it has manifested. You see, that is the difference between a prediction and a prophecy.

WHEN WAS THE BOOK OF REVELATION WRITTEN?
That leads to the third question: when was the book of Revelation written? Now for some of you this may seem kind of like an academic

exercise but put up with me for a few minutes. There are two main streams of thought here. Stream number one is that it was written in the sixties, and when I say the sixties I do not mean the 1960s, I mean the sixties of the first century. (A lot of people had visions in the sixties, too, but that is another sermon for another day.)

In the first century there was a man who was the leader of Rome by the name of Nero. Nero was a horrific man. In a sense, he despised Christianity, he despised the early church. He was such a tormented man that in the year A.D. 68 he actually took his own life. In A.D. 70 a man by the name of Titus, a Roman general, ransacked the city of Jerusalem, burned the Temple and began what we know as the Diaspora, or the taking of the Jewish people and scattering them throughout the world. They did not return until just a few years ago in 1948.

144

That being said, there are those who believe that John's description of the Temple found in Revelation 11 was actually describing the Temple of his present day. A few years later the Temple would be destroyed, so, basically, these people believe that the events in the Book of Revelation have already taken place. If they are correct, is their understanding considered prophecy or prediction? Their claim is a prediction because it is based on a particular person being in office and a specific building (the Temple) being in a specific place. These people claim that if the Book of Revelation was written prior to A.D. 70, then all of the events therein, except for the final judgment and thereon, have already occurred.

If the Book of Revelation was written after the reign of Nero, then the Apostle John was under the reign of a man named of Domitian when he received the revelation. This would have been in the late 90s, almost A.D. 96 or A.D. 97. This time period actually fits more with the situation because John was isolated on the island of Patmos. Nero did not isolate Christians. He soaked them in oil, lit them on fire and entertained his guests while Christians burned. Domitian took guys he did not like and sent them off to the middle of nowhere and said, "Welcome to the show Survivor! Have at it!" Do we find John burning at the stake? No. He is isolated on an island.

So, you may be wondering about those passages that speak of the revival of Rome and Babylon. These cities will be revived. What about the passage that defines the measurements of the Temple? Well, the Bible says there will be another Temple one day, no matter what the politicians say this will happen. This is prophecy, not prediction.

145

WHERE WAS REVELATION WRITTEN?

Revelation 1:9-10 says, "I John, who also am your brother, and companion in tribulation, and in the kingdom and patience of Jesus Christ, was in the isle that is called Patmos, for the word of God, and for the testimony of Jesus Christ. I was in the Spirit on the Lord's day, and heard behind me a great voice, as of a trumpet." I personally believe that John was on the island of Patmos during the reign of Domitian. During his exile, he was in the spirit on the Lord's day and the Lord allowed him to see things like they had never been seen before.

The Book of Revelation is a message written from an earthly perspective, but it is also a message that we see from a heavenly perspective. Revelation 4:1-3 says:

After this I looked, and, behold, a door was opened in heaven: and the first voice which I heard was as it were of a trumpet talking with me; which said, Come up hither, and I will show thee things which must be hereafter. And immediately I was in the spirit: and, behold, a throne was set in heaven, and one sat on the throne.

And he that sat was to look upon like a jasper and a sardine stone: and there was a rainbow round about the throne, in sight like unto an emerald.

John is on the island of Patmos. The Lord comes to him and gives him a vision; it was not just a hallucination. In fact, Revelation 4 says that there was a point in time when the Apostle John is "caught up"—much like the Apostle Paul was in 2 Corinthians 12, and much like some of the other prophets of the Old Testament who were allowed to see the throne room of God. Here is what is so unique about the Book of Revelation—supernaturally, miraculously and prophetically the Apostle John is "caught up" or transposed so that he could see the future as if it is the present.

John has an incredible position. He is able to see the crystal sea with his own eyes. He is able to see the martyrs under the throne of God. He is able to see the cherubim and the seraphim worshipping the Lord in heaven and yet, at the same time, he is able to see the water turn to blood and the Antichrist install the mark of the beast. Yes, he is on the island of Patmos. Yes, the Lord comes to him while he is isolated in that time period. But somehow supernaturally, just like the Apostle Paul and others, he is transformed and transfigured and taken to a point and a perspective that none of us yet have had the privilege or the pleasure of seeing.

WHY DID GOD GIVE US THE BOOK OF REVELATION?

Who is the primary character of the Book of Revelation? Jesus Christ. What is Revelation? It is prophecy, not just prediction. When was it given to us? It was given to us after the destruction of A.D 70, so that we know it is prophetic and not just a prediction. Where did John receive the prophecy? John received the prophecy on the island of Patmos; but more importantly, in the heavens. That leads to the last and most important question: why would God give us the book of Revelation? What is so important about your life and mine? How is this going to change me today? Is this just going to fill my head with a bunch of knowledge so I can say I am smarter or maybe more intelligent than somebody else or will it truly impact me? Revelation 1:3 says, "Blessed 147 is he that reads, and they that hear the words of this prophecy, and keep those things which are written therein: for the time is at hand." This blessing is only offered in the Book of Revelation and does not occur in any of the other 65 books of the Bible. Now I am not suggesting that Revelation is more important or should have greater value than any other book of the Bible. I am just saying it is the only book of the Bible that says you will receive a blessing from understanding its contents. By the way, Esther is the only book of the Bible without the name "God" in it, and I would never demote it below other books. All of the books are of equal value because they all came from God Himself.

I hear a lot of teaching today on a blessed life. Do you want a blessed life? Then, go to the Book of Revelation. I hear a lot of people saying, "I need a blessing in my life." Then, go to the Book of Revelation. Let me tell you two things that understanding and studying the Book of Revelation will do for you. The first thing is this: it will change your attitude. Revelation says blessed is the one who reads and hears. That means you actually have to open it, read it, address it and study it. The second thing is that it will change your actions.

Change of Attitude

Do you know how studying the Book of Revelation will change your attitude? One of the things you will discover when you read Revelation is that everything you have worked for, everything you have strived for one day is going to end up in a ball of fire. It will show you that at the very end, when all is said and done, human government, human politics, human engineering is not what withstands time. It is the Lord Himself that withstands time.

If you are struggling with what you see out in the world then I have good news for you: read the Book of Revelation and you will discover that in the end, God wins! Those guys on television do not have a clue of what they are talking about. If you want to have a changed attitude, if you do not want to get sucked into the mores and morass of life, read Revelation. Have the book out when you are watching the nightly news and say, "No, they're wrong." Why? Because the Lord says that is not how it ends. The message of the Book of Revelation will change your attitude toward life. You will get out of the dumps; you will get out of depression, and you will stop thinking things like, "I cannot believe this world is doing what it is doing." Guess what Revelation says? It is going to get worse and you can literally say the

Lord told me this was going to happen. This will change your attitude and when your attitude changes, you receive a blessed, changed life.

Change of Actions

The truth found in Revelation will do more than change your attitude, it will change your actions. Blessed is he that reads and hears and keeps. What do you have to do? What are the things with which you should be proactive? Have a vigorous prayer life and a vigorous worship life. Proclaim the message and tell it on the mountaintops. Preserve the message and be proactive with our faith.

Let me sum this up in two simple statements. There are two things that I see people do when they study the Book of Revelation: issue number one—people "go crazy." They sell everything they have, go sit on top of a hill and sing Kum Ba Yah until Jesus comes back. Turn those guys off! Do not join their club and do not move into their houses. That is the crazy response.

Most of you are not going to fall into that camp, but let me tell you where some of you are going to fall. When you start reading the Book of Revelation, studying it and you find out about the tribulation, the Antichrist and the like, you do not go crazy, you suffer from what I call caveman syndrome. You build yourself a cave and you hide in it. And you take on the theology of Chicken Little saying, "The sky is falling, but it won't fall on me."

The Bible says we are to "keep." Revelation 22:6 describes a very proactive faith. Let me tell you how you know if you are getting the purpose of the Book of Revelation: if it makes you more excited about serving the Lord, you have an understanding of Revelation. If it makes you more thrilled to give to missions, you get the message of Revelation. If you see people as an eternal destiny and not just someone who is in your way, you get the purpose of the Book of Revelation. When you do not build a cave, you do not go sit on a mountaintop, but instead you take the breath God gave you, the resources God gave you and say it is time to get serious about this thing that I call Christianity, then you get the message of Revelation! The time is at hand. Do not go crazy, do not go into a cave. Do something with what God has given you because the time is at hand. If we ever steer from who the person of Jesus Christ is then we have missed everything.

The Book of Revelation is not just about seven years known as the tribulation; it is not just about an Antichrist, a millennium or Armageddon. Let me tell you what it is about: it is about the fact that every one of us has sinned, that Jesus Christ loved us enough to go to the cross for us, to die for our sins and to arise from the dead so we do not have to experience the traumatic events in the Book of Revelation. We can be saved, redeemed and born again. When you get back to full circle, it is just about Him.

Chapter 9

Is America in Revelation?

The vision given to John is eclectic. There are nations and rulers. There are judgments and there is a remnant. But there is also something very unique. With the future of the universe at stake, the unthinkable occurs. That which was thought extinct is revived. Places of ancient times are once again lands of prominence. Countries that had once been relegated to history find themselves vibrant and thriving again. Rome is back. Babylon is back. Israel is back. The Middle East is the center of the world again, but.... is America in Revelation?

Have you ever wondered how the United States of America fits into the story of Revelation? Some of you may think that is a very egotistical, ethnocentric, narcissistic question. Although 194 other countries exist on planet earth, though there have been empires, rulers, and influence in other countries, history tells us that there has never been an entity that has been as powerful and prosperous as the country known as the United States of America. So, is America seen in the Book of Revelation?

Revelation 12:14—one single, solitary verse—makes an allusion to an animal, a bird. Those who claim that the nation known as the United States of America has a prominent role in the Book of Revelation and all the end time events look to Revelation 12:14 as their basis for such a belief. Revelation 12:14 says, "And to the woman were given two wings of a great eagle, that she might fly into the wilderness, into her place, where she is nourished for a time, and times, and half a time, from the face of the serpent."

So, who is this woman, who is this serpent, and who is this eagle? Those who want to advocate the prominence of the United States, not just in today's world but in the world as it is described in the Book of Revelation, claim the great eagle that comes and swoops up the woman and cares for her is the United States of America.

Before you get too excited about that proposal, allow me to take you back in history about two and one-half centuries ago to a time when this country decided on the official bird of the Untied States. At first, the

153

wild turkey received a unanimous vote. But, then our founding fathers realized that if the wild turkey was the official bird of the country, then no one could have turkey for Thanksgiving! Everybody knows bald eagles taste bad! So, there we have it . . .the bald eagle is our national bird. I make light of that story, but just to say that our national bird is an eagle, therefore the eagle found in Revelation represents America is a frivolous argument.

Revelation 12:1-17 says:

154

And there appeared a great wonder in heaven; a woman clothed with the sun, and the moon under her feet, and upon her head a crown of twelve stars: And she being with child cried, travailing in birth, and pained to be delivered. And there appeared another wonder in heaven; and behold a great red dragon, having seven heads and ten horns, and seven crowns upon his heads. And his tail drew the third part of the stars of heaven, and did cast them to the earth: and the dragon stood before the woman which was ready to be delivered, for to devour her child as soon as it was born. And she brought forth a man child, who was to rule all nations with a rod of iron: and her child was caught up unto God, and to his throne. And the woman fled into the wilderness, where she hath a place prepared of God, that they should feed her there a thousand two hundred and threescore days. And there was war in heaven: Michael and his angels fought against the dragon; and the dragon fought and his angels, And prevailed not; neither was their place found any more in heaven. And the great dragon was cast out, that old serpent, called the Devil, and Satan, which deceives the whole world:

he was cast out into the earth, and his angels were cast out with him. And I heard a loud voice saying in heaven, Now is come salvation, and strength, and the kingdom of our God, and the power of his Christ: for the accuser of our brethren is cast down, which accused them before our God day and night. And they overcame him by the blood of the Lamb, and by the word of their testimony; and they loved not their lives unto the death. Therefore rejoice, you heavens, and you that dwell in them. Woe to the inhabiters of the earth and of the sea! For the devil is come down unto you, having great wrath, because he knows that he hath but a short time. And when the dragon saw that he was cast unto the earth, he persecuted the woman which brought forth the man child. And to the woman were given two wings of a great eagle, that she might fly into the wilderness, into her place, where she is nourished for a time, and times, and half a time, from the face of the serpent. And the serpent cast out of his mouth water as a flood after the woman, that he might cause her to be carried away of the flood. And the earth helped the woman, and the earth opened her mouth, and swallowed up the flood which the dragon cast out of his mouth. And the dragon was wroth with the woman, and went to make war with the remnant of her seed, which keep the commandments of God, and have the testimony of Jesus Christ.

155

WHEN DOES REVELATION 12 TAKE PLACE?

In Revelation chapters 4 through 19 we have a portion of scripture that is dominated by the time period known as the great tribulation, that seven years of history that is called Daniel's Seventieth Week and Jacob's Trouble. During all of those tribulation events happening on earth, there are four chapters of Revelation that are parenthetical. Parenthetical means that the Biblical passage is literally extracted from the actual chronology of the portion of scripture in which it finds itself. Revelation 7, 10, 12 and 14 are parenthetical chapters. For example, Revelation chapter 7 talks about those of every tribe and nation who worship before the throne of God. Also, Revelation chapter 10 talks about the little book that John is told to eat but never revealed.

Now the reason for a parenthetical is this: the Lord gives us a parenthetical chapter, removes us from the chronology and from the minutia of all that is happening so that we can get some background information or some future foresight into how all of the events will play out. In fact, what we see in Revelation 12 is definitely beyond the chronology, 156 not only of the tribulation but of the Book of Revelation because it describes both the incarnation of Jesus up to His ascension and even beyond that to the final war in all of heaven. In order to understand when Revelation 12 occurs, we must first realize that it is a parenthetical chapter. You see, Revelation 12 is taken out of the chronology to give us the big picture.

Revelation 12 takes place in the last part of what we know as the great tribulation. In fact, it is very verbal and worrisome to say this, but Revelation 12 actually occurs after what we know as the abomination of desolations. Jesus prophesied in Matthew 24:15 that there would come a day where an entity known as the Antichrist would go into the Temple (which one day will be rebuilt) and offer a sacrifice that is not ordained by God. At that point he will reveal himself, not as a helper of humanity, not as a savior of mankind; but he will reveal his true nature—he is the devil incarnate, he is the enemy of humanity disguised as one who came to help but who has actually come to hurt. In Matthew 24:16 Jesus says when you see this happen to run to the hills, run to the mountains because when this event occurs you better look out!

WHO ARE THE CHARACTERS OF REVELATION 12?

Notice, if you will, what happens in Revelation 12:13-16. The person known as the "woman" is literally fleeing for her life. The event known as the abomination of desolation most likely happens somewhere right in the middle of the tribulation time period. I say all of that to say this: we cannot pinpoint exactly when Revelation chapter 12 is happening because it is not a chronological chapter within the great tribulation. We have to understand that in Revelation 12, particularly verse 14, we are at the end of that event and that time period known as the great tribulation. Here is where it gets really good: who are the characters, who are the people that are involved? After all, if it is the eagle on two wings that rescues the woman from the serpent who are all these people and why are they doing all that they are doing?

Definitive Characters

I want to begin with two entities or two characters that are not disputed; they are very definite characters. Chapter 12 involves seven different characters but there are three main ones. There is the woman, there is the dragon or the serpent, and there is the man child. The eagle is actually arbitrary. So let's talk about the two that are definitive.

One absolute definitive character or the entity is Satan. In fact, almost every Biblical description that he falls under is found in Revelation chapter 12. He is called the great red dragon, the serpent, that old devil, the accuser; it is almost as if the Lord is saying do you understand who this guy is? There is no disputing, no arguing that the dragon who waits on the birth of this child is Satan himself. His name means accuser; the Bible says that he accuses the brethren. The Bible says that he throws one-third of the stars out of the sky. He makes war with Michael and his angels. We cannot dispute or argue the identity of that character.

There is a second definitive character, the man child who comes out of the woman whom the dragon wants to devour. When you look at the text you realize this character has to be Jesus Christ. Why? Because Revelation 12:5 says, "And she brought forth a man child, who was to rule all nations with a rod of iron: and her child was caught up unto God, and to his throne." Not only does that describe the totality of the ministry of Jesus in one single verse, but I think we would testify that the birth of Jesus, the life of Jesus, the cross of Jesus, the resurrection of Jesus, the ascension of Jesus and the return of Jesus is the one thing that the serpent Satan despises more than anything because it is this man child, Jesus, who determines once and for all his eternal destiny—the lake of fire.

Debated Character

Those are definitive characters. We know the dragon is Satan. We know that the man child is Jesus. But then there is that debated person: who is this woman? The woman in Revelation 12:14 is taken care of by the two wings of the eagle. The woman is flown out, protected, and provided for. We need to understand that the woman represents a particular group of people.

Now there are three main thoughts on the identity of this woman. One of the main thoughts that has been propagated throughout the years is that the woman is Mary—the one whom we celebrate at Christmas time with the birth narrative, the Magnificat. Because she is the one who travails and delivers the man child, this woman must be Mary. This idea is taught in multiple religions throughout the world. However, there are several problems with this theory. One of which is in Revelation 12:6 which says, "And the woman fled into the wilderness, where she had a place prepared of God that they should feed her there for (three years)." Nowhere in scripture do you find Mary fleeing into the wilderness from the face of the dragon for three years. She and Joseph take Jesus into Egypt, but they did that for two years, not three. Revelation 12:13-16 says that during the time that the woman is in the wilderness that God supernaturally fed her. Now I have to ask the question: If Mary is the woman, then what about poor Joseph? Did he go three years without any food at all? Every man I know is not going to let that happen. We are going to make sure that we eat. The Bible says that she is fed for three years, and I believe that is a supernatural feeding. I think we can remove from the table the concept of the woman being Mary.

The second idea, and I think there are good intentions behind this, is that the woman in this story is the church. The main problem with this concept is that in this story the woman gives birth to the child. The New Testament does not teach that the church gives "birth" to Jesus.

159

Jesus gives birth to the church. If it were not for the life of Jesus, there would be no church. If there were no cross of Jesus, there would be no church. There never was a church until Jesus arose from the dead! Now we can be the called out ones. Now we can be saved. Now we can be called a part of the redeemed. We did not birth Jesus; Jesus birthed us!

So, if the woman is not Mary, and if the woman is not the church, we are really left with one final option. The person known as the woman in Revelation 12 is Israel, the people of God. To begin with, Revelation 12:1 says that she has the sun and the moon under her feet and a crown of twelve stars around her. Genesis 37 tells of the dream of Joseph, Jacob's son, one of his many children. Joseph has a dream that his eleven brothers bow down before him. In Genesis 37:9-10, the dream of Joseph, we see the moon and sun under Joseph's

> *This is why Revelation 12 is so important: the eagle is an entity that harbors and protects the interests of Israel, the people of God.*

160

feet and the stars, representing his brothers, worshipping him. There would be some who would say Joseph had eleven brothers but there are twelve stars in the dream. Yes, because Joseph was not Israel; Jacob, his father was Israel. And if you count him in the mix, instead of eleven, you have twelve.

Who was it that birthed the Messiah known as Jesus Christ? I know that Mary had a vital part in that role; and I know that the Messiah, Jesus, birthed the church. But you have to understand that the Bible says that Jesus was born of the seed of David, he was born of the seed of Abraham. In fact, the Apostle Paul speaking to Gentiles said that

He (Jesus) came to the Jew first. In fact, John chapter 1 says that He came unto His own, but His own rejected Him. Read Matthew chapter 1 and every person listed in the genealogy of Jesus is a God-fearing Jewish man or woman. It is the nation of Israel; the people of God travailed for thousands of years until the man child, Jesus, was born. This is why Revelation 12 is so important: the eagle is an entity that harbors and protects the interests of Israel, the people of God.

WHAT HAPPENS IN REVELATION 12?
A Procedure

The next question is this: What happens in Revelation chapter 12? After the abomination of desolations, after the Antichrist character comes to power, a procedure takes place which very much parallels an Old Testament story that is still celebrated today by the Jewish people known as the Passover. The people of Israel are in trouble. In fact, they are going to be destroyed; they are going to find themselves in a situation that is not pleasant whatsoever. They do not have food; they are on the run and yet the Lord provides for them in the wilderness. The person known as the dragon, or Satan himself, is trying to destroy the people of Israel. That is the procedure—a group of people on the run for their lives.

A Parallel

So what is the parallel? The parallel is the most famous story in Israel history: the exodus. Remember there was a time period in the Old Testament where there raised up a pharaoh who knew not Joseph. There is a ruler who is good, kind and generous and then in a moment, in

Simple

a twinkling of an eye, there is one who puts them in slavery, just like you see in Revelation 12. Everything is going good at first and then, suddenly, things take a turn for the worse. We would have to testify that the person known as pharaoh did everything he could to destroy the people of Israel in the Old Testament. But, God rescues them with the parting of the Red Sea, and He delivers them into the wilderness where they are supernaturally fed for forty years of existence. Do you notice the parallel here?

Let me tell you something: if you want to know how to live today read your New Testament, if you want to know what is going to happen tomorrow read your Old Testament because history always repeats itself. Those of us who refuse to learn from history are doomed to repeat it. What happens in Revelation 12? You have a procedure of these people known as Israel, the woman, fleeing for their lives and it is an exact parallel to the exodus story.

WHERE DOES REVELATION 12 TAKE PLACE?
A Place of Possession

The next question is this: Where does Revelation 12 take place? Notice what Revelation 12:14 says, "The woman were given two wings of a great eagle that she might fly into the wilderness, into her place." The Bible does not say that the woman goes to some random wilderness; it does not say that she just finds a convenient spot and stops there. Instead, we notice that there is a possessiveness to the place of her refuge; the Bible says she goes to *her* place.

Can I be honest with you? If you were to ask me where, specifically, is that place to which the woman flees, I would have to respond with my four favorite words when it comes to Revelation: I do not know! But I do have an idea because in the history of the Israeli people there are two specific places where the Lord has taken care of them in a magnificent fashion. One is what I would call ancient history, what we know as the situation of the exodus where they were taken out of the Red Sea into the wilderness and for forty years they were cared for. Their shoes did not wear out. (Sorry women, they wore the same pair for forty years.) Their clothes did not wear out; they stayed in style the whole time. And they were supernaturally fed with Krispy Kreme doughnuts every morning for forty years! (Well, the Bible does describe the manna as round, sweet and tasty. Not to mention it is only good for one day. We all know Krispy Kreme is only good on the day in which you buy them!)

163

The woman is protected. But it was in the wilderness that she was protected. Maybe during this time period the people of Israel flee back to the place where they were last protected. I do not know. But notice the Bible does not say a wilderness or even *the* wilderness; it says *her* wilderness.

In a little more modern history there was a time period in the first century when the Israelite and Jewish people were highly persecuted by the Roman government. They were exiled from the city of Jerusalem. Everyone tried to get rid of them to the best of their ability. There was a mountain region just south of the Dead Sea. (If you have ever wanted to see what a wilderness looks like, that is a wilderness. No trees; just desolation.) There is a mountain there by the name of Masada. For three years the Jewish people stayed in that place, protected from the Roman army until they finally came and got them. They ate from the food that was stock-piled there by the Roman emperor who preceded the current emperor. For three years they were protected with water that came in a unique fashion and food that was already there.

To this very day in the nation of Israel every man and every woman, (and yes, both genders have to serve) when they are commissioned into the Israeli military they are taken on the top of the mountain of Masada, and they are given a Torah, a copy of the first five books of the Old Testament. The commissioning ends with a statement: When all else fails, Masada will stand. In other words, if worse comes to worst, come to Masada. Could it be that during this time spoken of in Revelation 12, that the Israelites go to the original wilderness? Or, do they go to Masada? I do not know if it is going to be the exodus wilderness. I do not know if it is going to be Masada. I do not know if it is going to be another place. But I do know that according to Revelation 12, the Israelites will know. It is not like they have a big camp meeting and all the tribes get together and say where shall we go? The Bible says that they all flee to "her" place; it's a place of possession.

A Place of Provision

It is also a place of provision. In the parallel in Matthew 24 Jesus said they do not pick up any food. You remember the exodus story? Why did the Israelites eat unleavened bread? There was absolutely no time for them to make bread. They did not have time to get everything together and to allow the yeast to rise. They took what they had and left, and God took care of them. The same picture is here in Revelation

12. There is a place of possession, but it is also a place of provision and protection. For three years they do not have to worry about where the food is going to come from, where their protection is going to come from, and the Lord protects them in a supernatural way from a supernatural enemy.

WHO IS THE EAGLE?

Finally, who is this eagle? In Revelation 12:14 the wings of the eagle take the woman, help her and provide her a way of escape from the dragon, who is Satan. So, who is or what is the identity of this eagle? There are many who would look at this passage and believe in light of the world's situation and the greatness of a country known as the United States of America, who uses the eagle as its national bird, that this "eagle" must be America coming to the aid of Israel. Can I be honest with you? What I am about to say is completely politically insensitive and unpopular, but it is Biblical. Listen to me clearly: Israel does not need us! We need them. The Bible says pray for the peace of Jerusalem, not for the peace of Washington D.C. The Bible describes the twelve tribes of Israel, not the twelve tribes of the beltway. Now I am all for voting, and I am all for being politically active, but you need to understand something: we may be the only country that ever votes with Israel, but we act as if Israel did not have America that they would be in a mess. Let me remind you of 1973, 1967, 1948, and Exodus, chapter 19: they do not need us! So, this idea that "if it is not for America, then poor Israel" is simply not right. Israel has done just fine for thousands of years, with or without the help of the United States. Understand this clearly, America needs to continue to be a friend to Israel because history teaches us that the Lord turns His back on every entity and every country that turns its back on Israel.

We are the ones in a mess if we ever decide to start turning our back on Israel. Thankfully, we are still voting with them; at least for now.

But that being said, who, then, is this eagle? You can interpret it in the light of politics, procedures, and such, but I think the best thing to do is interpret it in light of what the Bible says. Remember that parallel event back in the Book of Exodus when the Israelites are taken out of Egypt, across the Red Sea and into the wilderness? In Exodus chapter 20 there is the place where Moses comes and gives the Israelites the Ten Commandments. Now in the preceding chapter, in Exodus 19:4, there is a very emphatic statement. The Lord says through Moses do you not see what I did unto Pharaoh, how I bore you up on eagles' wings. In other words, the picture in the exodus, the parallel story, is that the Lord is making the statement that Israel did not need Egypt, Syria, Lebanon; they did not need anybody. The Lord was saying,

> I think it is a stretch to say that the eagle in Revelation 12:14 is America or anybody other than the Lord Himself.

166

"I am the One who supernaturally took care of you and provided for you." So, when you go back into Exodus 19:4 the picture of the wings of an eagle is not another country, no matter how benevolent they may be. The wings of an eagle picture a supernatural deliverance by God. There is a pillar of fire, a cloud, a Red Sea parting, and clothes not wearing out for forty years. No other nation came and provided for Israel with those means; God Himself did.

There is a second verse in the Old Testament, in the book of Isaiah chapter 40. It is a verse that we oftentimes see on posters and magnets. Isaiah 40 is prophesying about the redemption of Israel. It speaks about John the Baptist, it speaks about the millennial time period when the mountains will be brought low and the valleys shall be raised up. Then, there is that verse in Isaiah 40:31 that starts with a word I love so much: but. "But they that wait upon the Lord shall renew their strength; they shall mount up with wings as eagles; they shall run, and not be weary; and they shall walk, and not faint." In Isaiah chapter 40 there is no reference to any deliverer other than the Lord. In fact, when you study the prophets, whether it be Moses, Isaiah, Jeremiah, Ezekiel, Micah, Nahum, etc, you see that the people of Israel got into trouble when they trusted other nations to deliver them rather than the Lord.

I think it is a stretch to say that the eagle in Revelation 12:14 is America or anybody other than the Lord Himself. The eagle is not the United Nations; it is not a sovereign entity; it is not a group of people who get together to bring peace. I will tell you who it is: it is the hand of God! Only the hand of God can do what He does in Revelation 12 where He stops the flood, He puts it at bay, and He supernaturally feeds the Israelites.

167

This leads to some very interesting implications for us because as you study the book of Revelation, if chapter 12, verse 14 is what we have said it is, then you are incredibly hard-pressed to find any possible allusion or reference to America. After all, Rome is revived; Babylon is revived; Israel is revived. So what are the implications for you and me and for America? America is not specifically mentioned, and let me go ahead and say that does not mean that the country of America ceases to exist; it is just not the place of prominence that it is today. It is not the super power that it is today. You do not see, in the Book of Revelation, a scene where the Antichrist comes over across the Atlantic

Ocean to "hang out" with the President of the United States. You see him going into Rome and into Babylon. Once again, the Middle East is the center of the world. There is somewhat of a picture of a "blending in" so-to-speak; power is lost, prominence is lost, prosperity is lost.

Let me share with you the negative news: we are getting there quicker than you can imagine. Every day that goes by, there is less and less commitment to the things of God in our country. We are raising a generation of people twenty years of age and under where less than five percent of them even go to church on a regular basis. Just yesterday I had the privilege of walking on what we know as the USS Alabama, that battleship that served so valiantly in what we know as World War II. Do you know that during that era roughly fifty percent of our men and women regularly donned the doors of a church to worship? That means we have taken a ninety percent decline in just four simple generations. Let me share with you the negative news: the negative news is we are headed south quickly. The negative news is the prominence of America is not mentioned in the book of Revelation. The negative news—well, just watch the nightly news and you will see the negative news.

Is there any positive news whatsoever? Yes, there is and let me tell you why. In the midst of all that, the Lord always has a remnant. There is always a remnant; always a people who, when they turn to the heart of the Lord, the Lord turns to them. People ask me all of the time if I believe that the Lord could allow and cause a great revival to take place in our midst? I will tell you why I believe it can happen. Any time that an individual, a family or community turns their heart to the Lord what does the Lord do? He answers and He revives them and He heals them.

We can talk about America all day long. We can talk about politicians all day long. We can talk about the systems that we have adopted rather than a Savior. We can talk about America and the world powers, but if a revival is ever going to occur in this country, in this day, there is only one way that it will happen. Let me show you how. Take your finger, draw a circle around yourself and say, "It must start right here." We can spend hours analyzing, blaming and ridiculing when what we really need to do is spend hours getting ourselves right with the Lord so that others may follow our example.

We have considered things that in some ways are speculative and in some ways are curious, but there is one thing I do know: the Bible 169 says in Luke chapter 15 when one sinner repents, when one sinner recognizes they have strayed from God, when one sinner recognizes that Jesus Christ is Savior, when one sinner says, "I turn from my wicked ways, save me God," that the Father in Heaven rejoices, He celebrates, He saves and, He forgives. Would you be willing to draw a circle around yourself right now and say, "Let revival begin right here?"

Chapter 10

Jesus Christ

The heavens open up. A majestic voice speaks. John turns around to see a sight like none other. There is an individual standing before him. He has a robe down to His feet. His head and hair are white as snow. His eyes are burning as fire. His feet are as brass. There is a sword coming out of His mouth. His appearance is as the sun. John bows as if dead because this is not a dream. The man is not a figment of his imagination. It is . . . Jesus Christ.

Throughout the course of this study we have been walking through, journeying through, one of the most mysterious yet anticipated, as far as content is concerned, books of the Bible. We have studied various subject matters such as the time period known as the great tribulation, an event known as the final judgment, the millennium, the person of the Antichrist, and the concept of the Book of Revelation being prophetic rather than just simply being predictable.

Now we come to the main character of the Book of Revelation. In fact, the very first verse of Revelation says "The revelation of Jesus Christ." Yes, we can study the Antichrist. Yes, we can look at the millennium. Yes, we can talk about Armageddon, but if we neglect the person of Jesus Christ in the Book of Revelation then we have neglected the whole purpose of the Book of Revelation—that purpose is to reveal, to show, to put on display for us the person of Jesus Christ.

> *We find a scenario where John the apostle has a vision—he sees Jesus Christ like he has never seen Him before.*

As we go through the book of Revelation there are the famous seven seals, the famous trumpets, the vials, the Antichrist, the mark of the beast; but throughout all of the text of Revelation there is a picture of the person of Jesus Christ. In the latter chapters He is reigning on a throne. In chapter 19, He is coming out of the clouds at His majestic second coming. In chapter 12, He is doing battle with what we know as the red dragon, that character known as Satan. In chapter 5, He takes the book sealed with seven seals and then at the beginning of

173

chapter 6, He begins to open those seals in that event that we know as that great tribulation.

As we turn to chapter 1, we find ourselves on the island of Patmos with an individual by the name of John, one of the first apostles. He had a brother by the name of James, they were the Zebedees. They were fishermen by trade whom Jesus called to follow Him. It was in that latter part of the first century that John found himself cast to the island of Patmos by the Roman leader, Domitian. Before anything is ever written in Revelation, before the mark of the beast is discussed, before New Jerusalem is given its measurements, we find a scenario where John the apostle has a vision—he sees Jesus Christ like he has never seen Him before.

174 This is the same apostle whom the gospel of John calls the beloved disciple. This is the one who sat closest to Jesus at all of their meals. If there was anyone who had a good perspective, a good picture, and a good visualization of what Jesus looked like it should be John. And yet when Jesus shows up in Revelation it is a picture like none other; it is a perspective that John could never imagine—which gives proof to the truth that fact is greater than fiction every time.
Revelation 1:9-20 says,

> *I John, who also am your brother, and companion in tribula-*
> *tion, and in the kingdom and patience of Jesus Christ, was*
> *in the isle that is called Patmos, for the word of God, and for*
> *the testimony of Jesus Christ. I was in the Spirit on the Lord's*
> *day, and heard behind me a great voice, as of a trumpet,*
> *Saying, I am Alpha and Omega, the first and the last: and,*
> *What thou seest, write in a book, and send it unto the seven*

churches which are in Asia; unto Ephesus, and unto Smyrna, and unto Pergamos, and unto Thyatira, and unto Sardis, and unto Philadelphia, and unto Laodicea. And I turned to see the voice that spoke with me. And being turned, I saw seven golden candlesticks; And in the midst of the seven candlesticks one like unto the Son of man, clothed with a garment down to the foot, and girt about the paps with a golden girdle. His head and his hairs were white like wool, as white as snow; and his eyes were as a flame of fire; And his feet like unto fine brass, as if they burned in a furnace; and his voice as the sound of many waters. And he had in his right hand seven stars: and out of his mouth went a sharp two-edged sword: and his countenance was as the sun shines in his strength. And when I saw him, I fell at his feet as dead. And he laid his right hand upon me, saying unto me, Fear not; I am the first and the last: I am he that liveth, and was dead; and, behold, I am alive for evermore, Amen; and have the keys of hell and of death. Write the things which thou hast seen, and the things which are, and the things which shall be hereafter; The mystery of the seven stars which thou saw in my right hand, and the seven golden candlesticks. The seven stars are the angels of the seven churches: and the seven candlesticks which thou saw are the seven churches.

175

The vision Jesus Christ allows the Apostle John to see gives us some incredible insight throughout the entire content of the Book of Revelation as to how Jesus is pictured in the book.

Allow me to be clear, from the very beginning of this study of Jesus Christ as we see Him in Revelation chapter 1 you are going to see the word "different" many times. The picture of Jesus in Revelation 1 is very different from the picture of Jesus riding in a fishing boat or turning water into wine or taking bread and feeding five thousand people. But I want to be very clear about this: the word "different" does not mean that the person is different. The Savior we see in Revelation is the same Savior we see in the gospels. He is the same God; the Savior with a different picture. "Different" does not mean different as in another, but as in a different perspective or a different picture.

Who Is Pictured In Revelation 1?

176

> *John's response to Jesus in Revelation 1 should be the same response that we have toward Jesus.*

That being said, the very first question we need to address is this: Who is pictured in Revelation chapter 1? Now you may be thinking this is a simple question with an obvious answer. We know who is pictured—Jesus Christ. He is called Alpha and Omega, the beginning and the end. He puts His right hand out and says fear not, I am He who is alive forevermore; I have the keys to death and hell. Jesus Christ is the obvious answer, but what we see in Revelation 1 is an absolutely different picture of Jesus than what we have in the four gospels—Matthew, Mark, Luke and John. The picture of Jesus in Revelation chapter 1 is not the Jesus we see pictured when He is talking to Nicodemus or the woman at the well or the woman who has been caught in adultery. This is Jesus seen from a completely different perspective, a completely different picture. And today, you and I, in the twenty-first century, must respond to Jesus appropriately or we will face grave consequences.

When Is The Picture From Revelation 1 Given To Us?

The next question is very vital: When is this picture given to us? The Jesus pictured in Revelation 1 is a Jesus that is post-ascension and pre-physical second coming—this is a different period of time. Let me explore what that means. When you study the personhood of Jesus Christ, obviously, He has always been and will always be, but there was a point in history that we celebrate at Christmas known as the incarnation when He was born of a virgin. There was also a period of time when He lived thirty plus years as a sinless individual, when He died on a cross, and when He physically arose from the grave. According to Acts chapter 1, Jesus physically ascended up on high 177 and now, according to Hebrews chapter 7, He sits on the right hand of the Father to ever make intercession for us. According to Revelation 19, one day the heavens are going to open up and He is going to physically descend at the Battle of Armageddon.

You might ask, "Why is that so significant for us?" Do you realize that you do not live in the period of time prior to the ascension; you do not live on the other side of the second coming? Understand this: the picture that John received of Jesus is the same picture that you and I should have of Jesus. John's response to Jesus in Revelation 1 should be the same response that we have toward Jesus. Revelation chapter 1 refers to a very specific period of time—that period of time after the ascension and before the literal second coming; the same period of time that you and I live in today.

As we examine detail by detail the picture and perspective of Jesus Christ in Revelation 1, do not fall into the trap of saying, "But that was 2,000 years ago." Do not fall into the trap of saying, "I am not on the island of Patmos." Do not fall into the trap of saying, "The Book of Revelation deals with things in the future." Do you understand that the picture given to John of Jesus in Revelation is the picture that you and I need to have of Jesus? (And, by the way, Jesus does not have long, flowing blonde hair, blue eyes and a completely white robe like many of the artists' renderings we have seen on display.) The picture that we see is very different from the pictures we paint. The picture we see is very different from the ones we imagine. And maybe our response will be different as well if we understand the proper picture of Jesus. Who is pictured in Revelation 1? Jesus. When does Revelation 1 take place? Between the ascension and the literal second coming.

What Is Actually Given To Us In Revelation 1?

The third question is this: What is actually given to us? What is the picture of Jesus that we have in Revelation chapter 1? Revelation 1:13 says there is a garment all the way down to Christ's foot. In other words, there is a robe-type item of clothing. Now this is significant because Revelation 1:5 says, "Unto Jesus who is the faithful witness, and the first begotten of the dead, and the prince of the kings of the earth. Unto him that loved us, and washed us from our sins in his own blood." That simple verse describes the three "offices" of who Jesus was, is and will be. It describes Him as a prophet; it describes Him as a priest; it describes Him as a King. And yes, all three of those persons, all three of those offices wear a robe down to the feet.

Now for us to respond appropriately we need to understand the three "offices." Today in the twenty-first century, do we respond to Jesus as a prophet? Do we respond to Him as a priest? Do we respond to Him as a King? In the gospels, Jesus was a prophet. In fact, in John chapter 1, John the Baptist made the statement that Jesus would come after the likeness of the prophet Moses. In Deuteronomy 18:18 Moses said that the Savior would come in his likeness and after his manner. Everywhere Jesus went He was forth-telling; He was foretelling. He was describing and proclaiming truth at the same time He was speaking events that would take place in the days ahead, in the future. In the gospels—Matthew, Mark, Luke and John—Jesus is a prophet, He is a teacher. He is called Master; He is called Rabbi. By the thousands, people listened to every word He said.

The picture we have in Revelation 1 is of the great universal High Priest, and He alone determines our destination.

179

But, in Revelation 19 and 20, Jesus comes as a King. He is one who sits on a throne; He is one who rules from Jerusalem. He is one who establishes a theocracy that is basically completely controlled by God Himself. In the gospels Jesus was Prophet. At the end of Revelation at His second coming, He is King. In Revelation chapter 1, He is Priest. Why is that significant? Why should that change your perspective and your response to Him? A priest, by definition, is the bridge between you and God. A priest is the one who is able to take your soul and determine its destination. That is why Jesus made the statement to call no man your Father but God alone. Never place your trust, your soul, and your eternity in another human being whatsoever; turn it over to Jesus. He is the Priest. If He is the only one who can control your destiny, if He is the only one who can determine where you spend all of eternity, then that should change how we respond to Him. You see, this is about more than seeing a miracle take place and seeing someone healed and hearing a great sermon. The picture we have in Revelation 1 is of the great universal High Priest, and He alone determines our destination.

Revelation 1:13 says Jesus is girt about the chest with a golden girdle—there is a robe around His chest. In other words, the picture John gets and we need to have is magisterial. This is so significant and, once again, such a difference from the picture we have of Christ in the gospels. In fact, the gospels say in Mark 10:44-45 that Jesus came not to be served but to serve many and to give His life as a ransom for many. Probably one of the greatest scenes in all the gospels showing Jesus as a servant is in John chapter 13 at the Passover meal, which is now called the Last Supper. After the meal was over, Jesus leaned down, took a basin of water and began to wash the feet of the disciples. The significance of this passage is that Jesus took a towel from across the rope of His waist. He took it off His waist and He began to serve; He began to help. He began to wash the feet of His disciples in order to demonstrate servitude. In the gospels the towel is around the waist of Jesus. He is the servant; He is demonstrating and showing what God truly looks like to humanity, but in Revelation chapter 1 He is not the servant. We are the servants of Christ. The role has been reversed: in the gospels Jesus was demonstrating to John who He was; in Revelation 1, John is to serve who He is. The perspective is very different, it is completely contrasted. The robe is the robe of a Priest; the sash is one of majesty.

Revelation 14 says, "His head and his hairs were white like wool." I think one of the things we struggle with when we read the gospels is not the deity of Jesus but it is the humanity of Jesus. We could belabor many minutes and many hours on this topic. We struggle with the fact that God was wrapped in flesh. John 1:14 says that "the Word became flesh and dwelt among us." Philippians 2 talks about the fact that Jesus did not think it was strange to be equal with God but He allowed Himself to be conformed to the trappings of humanity and to flesh. In the gospels Jesus walked around and people said, "Is this not the son of a carpenter; is He not of this tribe; does He not belong to this family?" Allow me to tell you what Jesus looked like in the gospels. He did not look like the paintings that we paint. He looked like your normal, average Jewish man: most likely He had dark hair, a beard and He wore the traditional garb.

181

Yet in Revelation chapter 1 His hair is white. Everything about Him is white; there is a sense of majesty to Him. Does white hair suggest a picture that He is now old? No. In fact, He is in a resurrected body. In Daniel 7:9, God and Jesus are described as "the Ancient of days." There is no age to Jesus because He is God. He is the same yesterday, today and forever. Jesus is not pictured as a man who, though sinless, grew up and died on a cross. He is pictured as God eternal; He is pictured as infinite; He is pictured as one who not only created time but is outside of time. He is for always. He is not just a man who some call Rabbi. He is not one who just has a following of some dedicated people. He is God. His dress is different. The girdle is different. His head and hair are different, but He is still the same Jesus.

Revelation 1:14 describes Jesus' eyes: "His eyes were as a flame of fire." When you read through the four gospels, you will notice the eyes of Jesus were very distinct. He had a certain way of seeing those who were in need of compassion. When Jesus saw Bartholomew under the tree He called to him and said, "You are an Israelite without guile." When He saw the man who was brought through the thatched roof, He had mercy on him. Imagine the look in Christ's eyes when He saw the woman who was caught in adultery; it was one of love and compassion. When Mary anointed Jesus' feet with the oil and the others criticized her, imagine the look of compassion she saw in His eyes when she looked at Him. In the gospels Jesus' eyes are looking to and fro showing compassion, showing love.

But this is not the picture we see in Revelation. In fact, the picture
in Revelation shows His eyes as flames of fire. Do you know what that represents? Judgment. We are accountable for our sins; we are accountable for our rebellion. This is not the Jesus of the gospels trying to show us that God loved us and came to save us. This is the Jesus who already went to the cross, already rose from the grave and now stands in judgment of who we are and what we have done. So the question is this: is He your priest or are you trusting another?
Revelation 1:15 says, "His feet are like fine brass." Think, if you will, about the feet of Jesus in the gospels. His feet took Him from Jericho to Jerusalem, to the Mount of Olives, to the Garden of Gethsemane. They took Him to Golgotha, to the cross. Ultimately His feet were pierced on that cross for our sins. The feet of Jesus wore traditional sandals, they received dirt just like everyone else's feet. Christ's feet were always going into places of humility and service to others.

Notice that the feet of Jesus in Revelation 1 are much different. They are not pictured in sandals; they are not pictured dusty; they are not pictured humbly going to the cross. Revelation pictures Christ's feet as brass, having authority and judgment. The picture of Jesus in Revelation 1 is not one of a humble servant. It is one of authority; it is one of power. It is one of ability. When Revelation 19 says He comes back, He treads the winepress of the transgressions of man. It is not a picture of a humble servant but a picture of Jesus, who has come with power and authority.

Revelation 1:15 also says that His voice is the sound of many waters. Consider the conversations that Jesus had in the gospels. He tells the woman who was caught in adultery in John 8 to go and sin no more. He tells the Phoenician woman who come and asks for crumbs from the table, "I have seen no such great faith; no, not in Israel." He tells 183 the Centurion whose child has died on his watch, "Don't worry, just go back home, your son has been healed." He tells the little girl who has passed away, "Rise out of your bed." It is the voice of healing; it is the voice of compassion.

In Revelation 1, Jesus has the voice of many thunders. In fact, in Revelation chapter 5, when He begins to instigate the seven seals, His voice thunders out. It is the voice of authority. It is the voice of judgment. It is a much different perspective than we see in the four gospels.

Revelation 1:16 tells us that "He had in his right hand seven stars," which are the angels to the seven churches (Jesus addresses these churches in chapters 2-3). Consider, for a moment, the right hand of Jesus. With His hands Jesus took mud and placed it on a blind man's eyes and said, "Now you are able to see." With His right hand he took a sick little girl and a disdained woman and helped them up. With His right hand He took the elements of the last supper and served them to each of the disciples. His right hand was a hand of help; it was a hand of servitude; it was a hand of humbleness.

Yet in Revelation 1, we see Jesus holding seven stars in His right hand—showing us His control, His authority. You see, in the eastern world the right hand is considered the hand of authority, power and control. The Bible very explicitly says not merely His hands, but His right hand. When John falls as the feet of Jesus, what does Jesus do? He touches him with His right hand and says, "Fear not."

Revelation 1:16 also tells us that "His countenance was as the sun." Have you ever stopped to think about the countenance of Jesus in the 184 gospels? Everywhere He went those who were wealthy were attracted to Him. Those who were poor were attracted to Him. Those who were injured and sick were attracted to Him. Even those who were confident, like Nicodemus the religious leader, were attracted to Him. The Scribes, Pharisees, and Sadducees came to Him, each one trying to trip Him up by asking Him complex questions. The Bible says that lepers were attracted to Him, as well as lawyers. You see, Jesus' countenance was of such magnitude that everyone was attracted to Him.

Have you ever tried to stare at the sun? Do you gravitate toward it or immediately turn away? Obviously, you pull away because the sun is too bright. In Malachi 4 Jesus is called the Sun of Righteousness. In Matthew 17 Peter, James and John are taken to the Mount of Transfiguration and there, with Moses and Elijah, Jesus is transfigured before them—His clothes as bright and as white as the sun. The countenance of Jesus Christ, as seen in Revelation 1:16, is so bright and so majestic that one's eyes cannot even stare upon Him.

You see, the whole perspective of Revelation 1 is completely different than the perspective we see in the gospels. Jesus is preaching, teaching and healing. He is saying, "I am showing you that I am who I say I am. Would you follow Me to the cross?" In Revelation 1, Jesus has already been to the cross; Jesus has already risen from the dead. He is the majestic One; He is our High Priest; He is the One who has the ability to judge, not just with His feet, but with His eyes and out of His mouth—His countenance is as the sun. You see, we should view Jesus in this way every day of our lives. We should see Him as our Priest; our majestic One; the One who has the ability to judge.

> *The structures, the buildings we meet within are not the church—we are the church and Jesus is in the midst of everything we do!*

185

Where Does Revelation 1 Occur?

John is located on the Island of Patmos; he is caught up in the spirit. However, notice what the Bible tells us in Revelation 1:13, "In the midst of the seven candlesticks one like unto the Son of man." Revelation 1:20 describes these seven candlesticks as the seven churches. You see, in the gospels, Jesus is proclaiming, preaching and instituting the church. But, in Revelation 1, Jesus is in the midst of the church. The word church literally means "called out believers." Do you understand the different perspective that we are given in Revelation as opposed to the one that we receive from the gospel accounts? Understand this, those who lived during the days of Jesus' earthly ministry (as described in the gospels) could escape to a different city or town and wait for Jesus to leave instead of listening to what He had to say. If they did not like His message or His presence, they could just leave town. However, Revelation 1 teaches us that as a believer in Christ, as a child of His, there is no running away; there is no escaping. Jesus is in the midst of our lives; He is in the midst of our church.

Imagine how differently most of us would act if we knew that Jesus was with us, in the midst of our daily comings and goings. Can you imagine how differently we would talk if we knew that Jesus was there when we spoke to those people on the other end of the phone line? Would we do what we do if Jesus was physically standing there with us? I would dare say, "No!" Well, guess what? He is there! He is in the midst! You cannot say, "I left Jesus at church because I am at work right now."

186

You cannot say, "I am going to leave Jesus at Bible study so that I can go out with my friends." Understand this: He is in the middle of the candlesticks! If you are a child of God, if you are a believer in Jesus Christ, then you are the church. The structures, the buildings we meet within are not the church—we are the church and Jesus is in the midst of everything we do! He is in the midst of everywhere we go. He is in the middle of our lives. Once again, you see that the picture Revelation 1 gives us is very different from the picture we see in the gospels.

Why Have We Received Revelation 1?

We have examined who Jesus is in Revelation. We have looked at the time frame of the vision John receives in Revelation 1. We have discovered what Revelation 1 pictures, and we have determined where the vision happens. But why have we received the vision of Revelation 1? Allow me to take you back to the gospels for a moment. Consider how the people responded to Jesus Christ during His earthly ministry. They were amazed! They marveled at His miracles, they marveled at His teaching. The people were so amazed at the person of Jesus Christ that they literally left everything they had, they stopped everything they were doing, and they followed Him. The apostles responded this way; many others responded in a similar manner. They followed Jesus everywhere. They walked with Him. Yet, when Jesus was dying upon a cross, the crowds thinned out; very few people were there—they abandoned Him when they realized how difficult it would be to follow Him with their lives.

Notice what happens to John when he sees Jesus in this vision. He does not respond, as some in our culture would do, by saying, "Isn't that neat? How cool! That is so special." No! The Bible tells us that John falls at the feet of Jesus as if he is dead. John worships without singing. John worships without giving. John gives us the proper response, and we should respond to Jesus in the same way today. When we realize who Jesus really is, we should bow down before Him and say, "You have all of me—not just the me on Sunday, not just a portion of my life—You have it all." John fell as if he was dead because he realized that everything—his whole life—was wrapped up in the person of Jesus Christ.

One of the most significant things we see in Revelation 1 is when John falls as if dead at the feet of Jesus, Jesus says, "I am he that lives and was dead; behold I am alive forevermore, Amen; and I have the keys of hell and of death. Write the things which thou hast seen, and the things which are, and the things which shall be hereafter." Why is this significant? Does John argue with Jesus? Does John gripe? Does John say, "But why do they always get to do the fun stuff?" Do you hear John say, "Well, Jesus, you just don't understand. I don't have time for this." Or, does he say something like, "If it fits into my schedule maybe I will work it in." No! You see, when John got a proper perspective of Jesus, He did exactly what Jesus asked of him—no matter what. And, he fell down, worshipped and said, "If you want it written, it will be written." When we see Jesus as John saw Jesus, as Revelation describes Jesus, it gives us a different response than we often see in our culture. This is not the Jesus that we make into a celebrity. This is not the Jesus that we turn into a fad. This is not the Jesus that we market so that we can sell "Jesus" trinkets. This is the Jesus who is God in flesh, and He demands our utmost response.

188

Let me ask you a question: Do you know this Jesus or do you just know a Jesus who is convenient? Do you just know a Jesus who is your buddy? Do you know a Jesus as your BFF: best friend forever? Do you know a Jesus who, when you are in trouble, is convenient for you but when everything is going good in life you can do without? Or have you met the Jesus of Revelation 1? The Apostle John thought he knew what Jesus looked like. He sat closest to Christ at dinner time; he leaned on His chest—but when he gets to Revelation 1, he bows down as if dead and says, "You are Lord and You are in control of every aspect of my life." The most important question in all of life is this: Do you know Jesus? Do you realize that according to Revelation 1, Jesus has absolute control of your destiny and your eternity? How you respond to Him will determine everything.

Chapter 11

The Rapture

A voice sounds and it calls John upward. He is immediately in the presence of God and the angels. Patmos has become the throne room of God. This incident is the most debated topic regarding the book of Revelation both for its content and timing. Does it occur before the great tribulation, during the great tribulation, or after? Then the question is who? Why would someone be transported from the earth to the heavenlies regardless of being alive or dead? Is it just John or is this . . . the rapture.

As we have studied the Book of Revelation, we touched on many controversial subject matters; however, I believe we are about to deal with the most hotly debated, most highly discussed, most vigorously argued, and, oftentimes, the most fervent concept in all of the teachings from the Book of Revelation. Interestingly enough, our text for this area of study will come from the New Testament books of 1 Thessalonians and Matthew. If we are supposed to be studying the Book of Revelation, why are we focusing on other New Testament passages of scripture? I am glad you asked that question! You see, the subject matter—the concept known as the rapture—is not explicitly discussed within the Book of Revelation. In fact, that is one of the reasons why the rapture is so mysterious and so enthralling for people. Some people are adamant 191 that the rapture, in totality, happens before the great tribulation. Others are adamant that the rapture comes at the end of the great tribulation. And there are thousands of opinions that fall within those two particular camps of thought. I do find it interesting that the passages of scripture that most readily define and describe the event known as the rapture are not found within the Book of Revelation. We do, however, see in Revelation 19:11 that Jesus does split the skies, and the Bible makes it very clear that when He does physically return to earth the armies of heaven are behind Him. We do know at some point, whether in death or life, that we will join Him and we will return with Him.

As we dive into this study on the rapture, we are going to examine 1 Thessalonians 4:13 which, by the way, begins with my favorite word in the Bible, "but." Understand this, chronologically speaking, 1 Thessalonians is Paul's first letter. Roughly twenty years have passed since the ascension of Jesus. The early church has begun "getting on its feet" so-to-speak. First Thessalonians is the first portion of scripture that God gives to Paul and, indirectly, to us—the readers of the Word. Within this first portion of scripture we find passages that deal with the highly debated subject matter of the rapture. 1 Thessalonians 4:13-18 says:

> *But I would not have you to be ignorant, brethren, concerning them which are asleep, that you sorrow not, even as others which have no hope. For if we believe that Jesus died and rose again, even so them also which sleep in Jesus will God bring with him. For this we say unto you by the word of the Lord, that we which are alive and remain unto the coming of the Lord shall not prevent them which are asleep. For the Lord himself shall descend from heaven with a shout, with the voice of the archangel, and with the trumpet of God: and the dead in Christ shall rise first: Then we which are alive and remain shall be caught up together with them in the clouds, to meet the Lord in the air: and so shall we ever be with the Lord. Wherefore comfort one another with these words.*

192

One of the most interesting questions about the rapture is when does it occur? Allow me to say this from the beginning of our study—the fact of the rapture's occurrence and the people who are involved in the rapture is much more important than the time scale in which it occurs. I believe your personal belief about the timing of the rapture is a hill worth fighting for, but not a hill worth dying on. I think the events surrounding the concept of the rapture are more important than the actual timing of the rapture.

WHAT IS THE RAPTURE?
The Rapture Defined Hermeneutically

The term "rapture" is not found in any English translation of the Bible. Nor is the term "Trinity" found in the Bible. However, just because a specific English word is not found in the Bible does not mean that a concept, a principle, a teaching or a doctrine is not present within scripture. How, then, do we understand the concept of the rapture? The term "rapture" is defined hermeneutically. "Hermeneutics" is a theological term referring to a scientific, in depth process and conclusive study of scripture. Hermeneutics is important because studying scripture properly keeps us from making a verse mean what we want it to mean. In other words, when you study scripture properly, you have to compare verses to verses—you cannot simply make a verse say what you want it to say. You have to look at the context of the verses: such as when were they written, or when did the Lord inspire the writers.

> *Technically speaking, 1 Thessalonians 4:17 could read, "Then we which are alive and remain shall be (raptured) together with them in the clouds."*

193

What is the origin of the word "rapture?" Actually, this word comes from the concept found in 1 Thessalonians 4:17: "Then we which are alive and remain shall be caught up together." The phrase "caught up," or to be risen up, comes from the Latin word rapio, which is how we derive the English word rapture. Although I study the Bible in English, I preach the Bible in English, and I memorize the Bible in English, it is important to remember that the Bible was once written in other languages, Greek being one of them. Interestingly enough, the Greek word harpazo helps us to derive the English word "rapture." Technically speaking, 1 Thessalonians 4:17 could read, "Then we which are alive and remain shall be (raptured) together with them in the clouds."

When doing a broad study of scripture, we also find the word rapture in the Book of Acts chapter 8 in the first evangelistic message we have in scripture. A man by the name of Philip meets an Ethiopian eunuch, who is sitting in a chariot reading the scroll of Isaiah. The Ethiopian eunuch admits, "I do not know what I am reading. I do not understand it. How can I learn if I do not have a teacher?" Philip begins teaching the eunuch from the scroll of Isaiah and then he proceeds to tell him about Jesus Christ. When Philip finishes his "sermonette," or Bible study, he asks the eunuch what he thinks about Jesus. The eunuch responds by saying, "I believe Jesus is the Messiah. I believe that He is the Son of God." Philip asks what would hinder the eunuch from being baptized, and he baptizes him right there in the desert (that is a sermon for another day!).

194

The Bible tells us in Acts 8:38 that as soon as that evangelistic endeavor between Philip and the eunuch is over that Philip was caught up and taken away. He was harpazoed—he was raptured. Why is this important? It helps us define what it means to be "caught up in the air." We have an illustration of this when we see that Philip was in one place at one moment and in an instant he was supernaturally, by the hand of God, transported to a different place. In light of that, we can understand the rapture to be an event, an occurrence when a person is taken from one place to another in an instantaneous event.

The Rapture Defined Historically

It seems that every time I walk into a Christian bookstore and view books on the end times, eschatology, and the Book of Revelation there are numerous books concerning the concept of the rapture. You have seen the books—both fiction-based and factual—that discuss the phenomenon of the rapture. Historically speaking, however, the rapture doctrine has only been popular for about 200-250 years. If the rapture is of such importance, then why did it take so long for Christians to understand the concept?

Oftentimes the Church struggles, debates, argues and fights over theological issues. Quite frankly, sometimes we are just a little bit clueless. Throughout history there have always been strands, or roots of people, who have been spot-on when it comes to biblical doctrine; however, the masses of people oftentimes take a while to catch on. 195

For example, we would all agree that Jesus Christ is God in flesh. There has never been a time when Jesus did not exist. Jesus was God before His incarnation, Jesus was God in His incarnation, Jesus was God on the cross, and Jesus was God in the resurrection. Jesus was God in the ascension, and He is always going to be God. We understand that fact. However, do you realize that it took the Church 325 years to figure that out? It took 325 years for everyone to come to the table and say, "Yes, Jesus is God." Why? Because people were discussing the issue, debating the issue and arguing the issue. Even though there were those all along who agreed and understood that Jesus is God, it took a long time for the masses to come around to an understanding and an agreement.

Consider the Holy Spirit. The Holy Spirit is the third person of the Trinity: Father, Son and Holy Spirit. The Holy Spirit is who inhabits us when we are saved. The Holy Spirit gives us the power of righteousness and sanctification. The Holy Spirit, according to Romans 8:26, speaks on our behalf when we do not know how to pray. If it were not for the Holy Spirit, we would be in a mess! Did you know that the Church as a whole did not declare the Holy Spirit is God until 400 years after the time of Jesus Christ? We are slow learners, if you have not already figured that out! Historically speaking, it is important to understand that the literal when of someone's understanding of a particular Biblical doctrine is less important than the fact that he actually does understand and accept the doctrine.

The rapture is an event that includes the "catching away" of a group
196 in an instant, in a moment of time, and this doctrine has only been popular in recent days.

WHO IS RAPTURED?

The first thing I want to address is this: a specific group of people is raptured. The rapture doctrine, as we see in scripture, does not teach that all of humanity is raptured. Instead it teaches that the ones who are "caught up" is a specific group of people. There are others who remain.

Matthew 24:36-41 says:

> But of that day and hour knoweth no man, no, not the angels of heaven, but my Father only. But as the days of Noah were, so shall also the coming of the son of man be. For as in the days that were before the flood they were eating and drinking, marrying and giving in marriage, until the day that Noah

entered into the ark. And knew not until the flood came, and took them all away; so shall also the coming of the Son of man be. Then shall two be in the field; the one shall be taken, and the other left. Two women shall be grinding at the mill; the one shall be taken, and the other left.

Matthew is speaking in context about the return of the Lord in the big picture. The illustration we see in this passage of scripture is that there is a specific group of people who are "caught away" or transferred from one place to another. One person is taken and the other is left. First Thessalonians 4, 1 Corinthians 15, and peripheral passages in Revelation teach us that this "special" group of people taken, those caught up, those called out, are those who have established a relationship with Jesus Christ. First Thessalonians 4 makes a distinction between those who are dead in Christ and those who are alive in Christ. Those 197 who are alive in Christ have a "special" relationship with Him.

This "special" group of people—whether they are dead or alive—have understood that they were sinners, they strayed from God, they have spoken against God, and they have acted against God. They have understood their sin nature and have admitted their sin. They have also acknowledged that Jesus lived for them, died for them, and rose again for them. They ultimately have made the decision to ask Jesus to forgive their sin and save them. John 1:12 says whoever believes in Jesus shall become the sons of God; they become "special" when they are called of God.

For example, the name "Jeff" is a very common name. In fact, when I went to college I joined an organization of about 75 to 80 men, and there were five different individuals with the name "Jeff." Whenever someone in the group called the name "Jeff," either all of us or none of us named "Jeff" turned to listen. Quite frankly, over a period of about four years, while I attended school, I forgot my name was "Jeff" because everyone began to call me "Meyers." To this day, if Traci really needs my attention, she yells, "Meyers!" And I am there. You see the name "Meyers" now has an established, special relationship attached to it—in a sea of a hundred "Jeffs," when I hear the name Meyers, I know who it refers to—me.

Consider this as well; in a busy place, such as an amusement park, if you need to get your child's attention, a spouse's attention, or a friend's attention, you call his name. Several people with the same name might turn and look at you, but your child, your spouse, your friend knows you and he responds.

The scripture in Matthew gives us that picture. In this process, this event known as the rapture, there is a specific group of people called—not because they have been good, not because of the way they vote, not because of socio-economic levels or where they live geographically—but, they are called because they are sons of God and they have a relationship with Jesus Christ.

HOW DOES THE RAPTURE OCCUR?
A Quick Event

The rapture is not a long, drawn out process; it will occur very quickly. The Bible says that those who believe in Christ are immediately caught up in the presence of the Lord. In fact, 1 Corinthians 15:51

says, "I show you a mystery. We shall not all sleep, but we shall all be changed." 1 Corinthians 15:52 makes reference to "In a moment, in the twinkling of an eye" the mortal shall put on immortality, death loses its sting, those of us who are alive in Christ shall be changed and forever be with Him, and those who are dead in Christ shall be raised to forever be with Him. You see, there is a joining of the masses of the "special," the people of God, with the Savior, Jesus Christ.

Do you know that when you blink your eye one nanosecond of time elapses? A nanosecond is one one-millionth of a second. That is the twinkling of an eye! In fact, this may be the most important part of this entire study! I know a lot of people who use a lot of excuses to take their time on making a decision for the Lord. They say, "I'll get serious, I'll believe on Jesus when I see proof. I'll believe on Jesus when I understand more. I'll believe in Jesus when I have read this or that. 199 I'll believe in Jesus when this occurs. I'll wait until my kids are grown. I'll wait until this happens." Do you know that I have talked to people who actually have said if the rapture happens the way I believe it will happen, that then they will get serious about the Lord. They don't have enough time! One one-millionth of a second; you do not have time to blink, much less drop to your knees and believe in Christ! Believing in Jesus, accepting Him, must take place before the rapture, not simultaneously—there is not enough time for both to happen at the same time. The rapture is a very quick event.

A Quiet Event

Although contrary to popular movies from the 1970's and 80's—the movies with planes falling out of the skies, doctors vanishing, and other crazy events—the rapture is a very quiet event. Notice in the Matthew 24 passage, one is in the field, one is gone, one is left at the mill, and one is gone. The Bible tells us this event will happen like a thief in the night. Thieves typically do not make a lot of noise. Oftentimes it is even hours or days later before anyone notices that a thief has been around. First Thessalonians 5:2 says that Jesus comes as a thief in the night, and thieves are very stealthy and quiet. The thievery takes place quietly and the results are often seen later.

WHY IS THE RAPTURE DOCTRINE IN SCRIPTURE?

We all know that we are sinners. We all know that Jesus is the only means of salvation. The Bible speaks to the fact that He is the way, the truth and the life. The Bible tells us that one day Jesus is coming back; at Armageddon He is going to defeat Satan and all of His enemies. We know that Jesus is going to set up His Kingdom.

> *The rapture event is really a time to prepare you and me, those who have passed and those who are alive, for our future life with the Lord.*

200

One day there will be a final judgment. We know that if we believe in Jesus Christ then one day we will be with Him forever and ever, always in eternity. So, why did the Lord see fit that the rapture event would need to take place?

Now, understand this, I am not about to presuppose that I can get inside the mind of the Lord. According to the Book of Isaiah, His thoughts are higher than mind and His ways are higher than mine. But, allow me to present two thoughts based on the passages we have studied: the rapture prepares us for the future, and the rapture helps us deal with the past.

Preparing for the Future

We need to be prepared for the future, and the rapture event provides us with that preparation. Maybe you have not noticed this, but your body is breaking down. For some of you, your mind is going—some quicker than you realize! You see, we live in a broken-down, decaying, death-determining world, but the Bible tells us in 1 Thessalonians and 1 Corinthians that we will be changed—we will trade mortality for immortality! I do not know about you, but when Jesus comes back and fights the Battle of Armageddon, and I am in His army, if I have this body I am in trouble! Understand this, when the rapture event happens, the catching away, the taking up of the saints of God, the Lord is actually preparing us for the future by giving us a glorified body—that instant glorious body in which we will never grow old, never get tired and never need sleep. The rapture event is really a time to prepare 201 you and me, those who have passed and those who are alive, for our future life with the Lord.

Dealing with the Past

The rapture event helps us prepare for the future and it also helps us deal with the past. In 1 Thessalonians 4 Paul is encouraging the people not to be ignorant, confused or bothered by the passing away of those in the Lord. Remember, chronologically speaking, this is the first of Paul's letters. Imagine the anticipation of the people. Jesus has risen from the dead and witnessed to over 500 people. He has ascended before their eyes. The world is being transformed and changed immediately. The anticipation for His return during that day was much greater than our hope for His return. Yet, there are those saints of old who are passing away; there are apostles among them who are beginning to be martyred for their faith. Great men and women of God are dying and the people are wondering what is going on in their midst.

First Thessalonians 4:18 says, "Wherefore comfort one another with these words." It should give us great comfort that we will be united again with those who die in the Lord. Those in ancient days and those from our own relationships here on earth—spouses, moms, dads, brothers, sisters, aunts and uncles, cousins, friends and coworkers who had a saving relationship with Jesus Christ—will be with us in heaven with the Lord one day. Rather than believing there is no hope, rather than believing—as so many of the world do today—that you come to life, you die and then, that is it—nothing. The Bible tells us not to be ignorant or upset about those who die in Christ. We can comfort one another because we know that those who are dead in Christ, those who have passed away, will be with us one day in heaven. This helps us deal with losing loved ones. This helps us deal with losing friends. This helps us deal with the fact that one day our own lives will end— assuming the rapture does not occur while we are alive, our bodies will die. The rapture not only prepares us for the future, but it helps us deal with the past.

202

WHEN WILL THE RAPTURE OCCUR?
Now, allow me to be the first to say that there are a million different views on the "when" of the rapture. I believe that it is perfectly okay to agree to disagree. There are members of my family and my congregation who disagree with me and with each other over the timing of the rapture. You see, there are those who are absolutely adamant that there is no way whatsoever that the church of Jesus Christ will ever enter the

tribulation. In Revelation 6 through Revelation 19 there is no mention of the church. Jesus said, I will never leave you or forsake you, but it is Jesus who opens the seals that would cause forsaking; therefore, many believe Christians are raptured before the great tribulation.

Then, there are those on the opposite scale of the spectrum who read passages like Matthew 24, which comes on the heels of the abomination of desolations, stars turning colors and all kinds of other crazy events taking place, who believe that the people of God, the Israelites did not escape the persecution of God. They point to the fact that even the original apostles, except for John, were persecuted and martyred. These people believe that Christians will go through a great tribulation.

Then there is a third party who believes that Christians must go through a tribulation; however, Christians will not have to face the "really bad stuff." These people adhere to a pre-wrath rapture. Of course there are a thousand other views as well.

The problem with this whole doctrine of belief is that there are so many varying views over so many different times scales that at moments it all just becomes very muddy and unclear. At times it can seem like a holy war of doctrine.

I would like to present a possibility to you. In the course of my study over this topic, I read the book of 1 Thessalonians several times. Interestingly enough, there is nothing in the entire book of 1 Thessalonians that even hints at the tribulation. There is not a sniff of the Antichrist, not a hint of the mark of the beast, not even a clue of intense persecution.

The Book of 1 Thessalonians tells us that as we are going along in life, suddenly we will be caught up in the air, ever to be with Him!

But consider this, while Matthew 24 does not talk about the church or Thessalonica, Matthew 24 does discuss the tribulation. In fact, Matthew 24:15 talks about the abomination of desolations, fleeing for your life, running to the hills, the parable of the fig tree—as in the days of Noah. Matthew 24 is laced, from front to back, with all kind of ideas found in the Book of Revelation such as looking forward to Armageddon and dealing with the tribulation. Notice something, if you will: both passages of scripture, Matthew 24, which is very tribulation-minded and 1 Thessalonians 4, which is very non-tribulation minded, deal with an event where people are taken from one place to another.

204 Could it be that both sides of the argument are right? Now, I am not saying that two opposing sides can both be right about the same thing, but could it be that the pre-tribulation rapture of the church of Jesus Christ (what 1 Thessalonians 4 and 1 Corinthians 15 address), that time period before the tribulation, will happen for those who are dead in Christ and for those who are alive when He returns AND that those people who believe on the name of Jesus Christ during the tribulation time (those who are sealed on their foreheads with the seal of God), those 144,000, and those who come from every tribe, tongue, and nation will be raptured at the end of the tribulation in order to prepare for the Battle of Armageddon?

Allow me to show you a verse that may just blow your mind. Matthew 27:51-53, speaking about the death of Jesus, says:
And, behold, the veil of the temple was rent in two from the

top to the bottom; and the earth did quake, and the rocks rent: And the graves were opened; and many bodies of the saints which slept arose, And came out of the graves after his resurrection, and went into the holy city, and appeared unto many.

According to Matthew 27 there has already been a rapture. Is a rapture not a taking of a person, whether dead or alive, from one place to another? These people were dead! And when Jesus arose from the grave the Bible says they walked in the Holy City. Some people believe that the Holy City refers to the New Jerusalem, but the New Jerusalem is not in our midst yet! Throughout scripture the Holy City is the same as Jerusalem.

Acts 1:11 tells us that Jesus was on a mountainside with His disciples and He ascends into heaven. At that time, two angels make the statement "as He went so shall He return." He goes up, ascends in the clouds, and we see in Revelation 19 that He descends from the clouds. However, this is the interesting part! Does Jesus descend to the Battle of Armageddon alone? Revelation 19:11 tells us that He ascends with the armies of heaven; armies being plural! Could it be that in Matthew 27:52 when the many saints of old arose from their graves that they did so in order to ascend with Jesus Christ? We have no record that these people ever died again. Is it possible they ascended with the Lord?

I find it interesting that almost every time the Bible mentions resurrection, ascension or rapture that the Lord gives us agricultural terminology. Now, because I grew up in the city I did not spend very much time in agriculture. In fact, my wife and I have just experimented with our very first garden. I did not know that in a garden of eight by four feet you do not put in an entire bag of seeds! What started out as this cute little garden has taken over the entire yard! I am definitely learning about agriculture! However, there is something I do know about agriculture that is mentioned in scripture, and that is that we have three phases of agriculture. There is the first fruits, the harvest and the gleanings.

Could it be that those saints of old in Matthew 27 were the first fruits? Could it be that one day before what we know as the tribulation we have the harvest—2,000 years of those who have passed and those who are alive in Christ? And could it be that immediately before Armageddon there are the gleanings—those who come to know Christ in the tribulation?

206 You cannot escape the fact that the rapture passage in Matthew 24 is surrounded by tribulation language. You cannot escape the fact that the passages in 1 Corinthians and 1 Thessalonians are not surrounded in tribulation language. So how do we reconcile that? First, we reconcile it by not fighting so much about the "when" but concerning ourselves with the "who." And, the important fact is this: when this event occurs, whether my possibility is right or wrong does not matter. When the rapture occurs, Jesus Christ, Savior, God in flesh, resurrected and ascended on High, is going to come with the last trump! And when He sounds, those who are protected, those who are taken care of are caught up with Christ, not those who said, "God, I can do it on my own. I know a better way" or those who said, "I had perfect doctrine." Those who had a saving relationship in Christ will experience the rapture.

Is it important to study the "when" of the rapture? Absolutely. But it is more important that you know the "Who" of the rapture—Jesus Christ.

Chapter 12

The Mission

The great tribulation is escalating. The Antichrist is becoming more powerful. Hope is distant. Fear is rampant. But there are the faithful, those who refuse the mark and are sealed by God. Their existence is nomadic and one of seclusion but their message is not. They are mostly known by their number - 144,000. However, it is because of their faithfulness that every tribe and nation is represented in the heavens. This select group is not just a number, they are .... the mission

As we wrap up our study of the Book of Revelation, allow me to discuss with you why I have such fervor for the last book of the Bible. Oftentimes when I preach from the Book of Revelation I receive comments such as, "You seem like you are in the zone." Some people have made comments like, "You seem like this is where you love to be." Understand that my passion for studying end times truths actually, as many passions do, comes out of a sordid history, so-to-speak.

I know that I am not the eldest person around. In fact, I know that I have not seen all that many of you have seen. However, I had the unfortunate (or fortunate) privilege of growing up during some of the most tumultuous days in our American history. I know those days do not compare to the movement of the sixties and the rioting that took 211 place during those years, but I think all of us would confess that the decade of the seventies and the early eighties was a very tense time internationally, especially when it came to global affairs. No, I was not around during the Cuban missile crisis, however, surprisingly enough the early 1980s was actually the closest we ever came to nuclear war with our Cold War enemy, the Russians. I never knew life as a young child away from the Cold War, whether it was the Iran hostage situation or the Libyan invasion or all of the things associated with the Cold War. As a child, watching the news or listening to adults talking about our world created a very confusing and disturbing environment.

I experienced an event during my childhood that forever changed me. I was in sixth grade when one of our teachers had us break up into small groups to do a project. We were instructed to research the dimensions and all the necessary items needed in order to build a scale model of a nuclear bomb shelter. Now as a twelve or thirteen year old, imagine what goes through your mind when you going to school every day thinking you may not wake up tomorrow. Imagine what it felt like to wake up every day and watch the news coverage about all of the invasions and conflicts in the world. I began to wonder what was happening around me. Now, I was a believer in Jesus Christ; I had been saved for a couple of years but I was a baby—not only physically but also spiritually. As I saw the headlines, heard the news and went to school, I had a struggle going on within me. I had a hard time sleeping at night because I was paranoid about the world's events and everything that was happening around me. I literally felt that the sky could fall at any moment.

212 As those events began to progress, I went to a wise individual in my life (the one who this book is dedicated) and shared with him my struggle. He asked me this simple question: "Have you ever read the Book of Revelation?" I responded by saying, "No, I've heard about it. I know it's at the end of the Bible, but I just don't think I can understand what it means." He said, "Why don't you read through the Book of Revelation in one sitting and then come back and let's talk about it."

I'll never forget the night that I sat down with the Book of Revelation. I read it from front to back, and I did not feel like I learned one thing! I could not understand anything.

I went back to this mature friend and said, "Dave, I read it and I don't get it." He said, "Let me ask you a simple question. In the end, who won?" "Well, God did," I said.

To which he responded, "Exactly. Do you understand that in all these news stories you are seeing on television that people think they know how things in this world are going to work, but they really do not know the truth? They tell you that the world evaporates in a nuclear holocaust, but according to the Book of Revelation, is there a nuclear holocaust?"

They say that if the doomsday clock strikes this Tuesday without a debt deal on the table the world is falling apart. Do not listen to them. When you study the Book of Revelation, what you find out and discover is that most often what humanity says will be our demise, our end and our downfall, is much different from what the Lord says. You see, God is in control. He is in charge, and He knows how the world will end.

You and I live in a world today that is saturated with negativity and news regarding humanity and our efforts. People are saying that if 213 we continue driving cars the whole environment is going to implode. We have all heard different scenarios about our world's demise. We should have discussions about current events and how they affect our lives; however, understand that all of those scenarios and hypotheses we consider and debate have been devised by man. God has given us the Book of Revelation to tell us, "I am the One who opens the seven seals. I am the One who allows these things to occur. I am the One who ultimately has control of the end."

So you may be wondering to yourself, "Why is it that the end of this study finds itself in Revelation chapter 7 rather than at the end of the book in Revelation chapter 22?" Well, the reason I wanted to end this study with Revelation chapter 7 is because we work with people, we live next door to people, and we talk with people who are in desperate need of the truth. Our family, friends, strangers, and those who are moving into our communities need to know the gospel message. Possessing knowledge about the Antichrist and how he compares to Jesus Christ is great. Knowing how the millennium compares to the New Heaven and the New Earth is wonderful head-knowledge. But, ultimately we spend more time outside of the church walls than we do inside the church walls. Revelation 7 gives us our marching orders. From this chapter we learn what we should do now, and tomorrow, with what we have learned from the Book of Revelation.

Revelation 7 says:

214

And after these things I saw four angels standing on the four corners of the earth, holding the four winds of the earth, that the wind should not blow on the earth, nor on the sea, nor on any tree. And I saw another angel ascending from the east, having the seal of the living God: and he cried with a loud voice to the four angels, to whom it was given to hurt the earth and the sea, Saying, Hurt not the earth, neither the sea, nor the trees, till we have sealed the servants of our God in their foreheads. And I heard the number of them which were sealed: and there were sealed an hundred and forty and four thousand of all the tribes of the children of Israel. Of the tribe of Judah were sealed twelve thousand. Of the tribe of Reuben were sealed twelve thousand. Of the tribe of Gad were sealed twelve thousand. Of the tribe of Aser were sealed twelve thousand. Of the tribe of Nephthalim were sealed twelve thousand. Of the tribe of Manasses were sealed twelve thousand. Of the tribe of Simeon were sealed twelve thousand. Of the tribe of Levi were sealed twelve thousand. Of the tribe of Issachar were sealed twelve thousand. Of the tribe of Zabulon were sealed twelve thousand. Of the tribe of Joseph were sealed twelve thousand. Of the tribe of Benjamin were sealed twelve thousand. After this I beheld, and, lo, a great multitude, which no man could number, of all nations, and kindreds, and people, and tongues, stood before the throne, and before the Lamb, clothed with white robes, and palms in their hands; And cried with a loud voice, saying, Salvation to our God which sitteth upon the throne, and unto the Lamb. And all the angels stood round about the throne, and about the elders and the four beasts, and fell before the throne on their faces, and worshipped God, Saying, Amen: Blessing, and glory, and wisdom, and thanksgiving, and honor, and power, and might, be unto our God for ever and ever. Amen. And one of the elders answered, saying unto me, What are these which are arrayed in white robes? and whence came they? And I said unto him, Sir, thou knowest. And he said to me, These are they which came out of great tribulation, and have washed their robes, and made them white in the blood of the Lamb. Therefore are they before the throne of God, and serve him day and night in his temple: and he that sitteth on the throne shall dwell among them. They shall hunger no more, neither thirst any more; neither shall the sun light on them, nor any heat. For the Lamb which is in the midst of the throne shall feed them, and shall lead them unto living fountains of waters: and God shall wipe away all tears from their eyes.

215

Most of us are familiar with, at least in numerical value, the famous number 144,000 mentioned in the Book of Revelation. There are various groups, both past and present, who claim to be a part of this group. I am interested in diagnosing who is or is not a part of the 144,000, but I am more interested in the manner in which the 144,000 operate and live within the midst of the situation in which God places them.

WHO ARE THE 144,000?

Various groups of people that come and knock on your door, typically in pairs or in threes, will claim that they are members of the 144,000. In history, we have the Jehovah Witnesses, and from the early days of the Church of Christ, we have the Branch Davidians, as well as many other groups who have come forward and claimed to be the 144,000 described in the Book of Revelation.

A Distinct Group

216

Debates, discussions and arguments surround the idea of who makes up this group of 144,000. First and foremost, we need to understand that this is a very distinct group. What I mean by distinct group is that the group cannot be comprised of one set of people on one hand and another set of people on the other hand. Some individuals believe this group of 144,000 is symbolic of all of those people who have believed on the Lord through the ages.

You know, every now and then the Lord uses a theological two-by-four to hit us over the head, so-to-speak. As you read through Revelation chapter 7, the lists of the twelve thousand tribes may have become tiresome to you. Consider this thought: If the Lord tells us twelve times in a row that there were twelve thousand of twelve tribes then maybe we ought to realize that the 144,000 is twelve thousand of the twelve tribes.

It is like the Lord is saying, "How much more do I need to tell you?" The repetition is not merely redundant for no reason. The 144,000 is a very distinct group and is not a symbolic group of people. In fact, if someone claims to be a part of the 144,000 then simply ask that person, "Which tribe are you from?" Revelation chapter 14 alludes to the 144,000 and tells us that the 144,000 is a group of men who have never had intimate relations with a woman. So, an individual who is married cannot be part of the 144,000, and a person who is a female cannot be part of the 144,000. The number, 144,000, is precise; there are twelve thousand from the twelve tribes of Israel, and Revelation chapter 14 describes the group as only males who are lacking a marital relationship. Such a precise group is very distinct and different from the majority of people who claim to be a part of the 144,000.

217

A Different Group

Interestingly enough there is one group of people who claim they are descendants from the tribe of Ephraim. Ephraim was one of the original twelve tribes of Israel, but if you will notice, the twelve tribes listed in Revelation chapter 7 are actually different than the tribes listed in the Old Testament. You see, there are two tribes that are not listed in Revelation chapter 7: the tribe of Dan and the tribe of Ephraim. Old Testament history teaches us that those tribes fell into apostasy and idolatry. In the Book of Revelation, when the tribes resurface, Dan and Ephraim are not mentioned. However, modern groups—great in number—claim they are from the tribe of Ephraim for the latter days. The only problem with this fact is that when you read about the latter days in Revelation 7 there is no tribe of Ephraim listed.

In fact, two tribes have replaced Ephraim and Dan: the tribe of Joseph and the tribe of Levi. Old Testament history teaches that the Levites (the priests, the pastors, those who offer up the sacrifices for the people of Israel) were not to be landowners. They did not have what we would call a secular job. In fact, this is where we get the concept of giving a tenth of our income, or a tithe; it was given to the temple so the Levites could have their basic needs met. In Revelation 7, the Levites are numbered among the twelve tribes, whereas in the Old Testament they were in addition to the twelve tribes. The Levites were a special, set-aside tribe. So when we examine the 144,000, we need to remember it is a distinct group of people and a very different group of people.

WHAT ARE THE 144,000?

The first thing you need to understand is that the 144,000 is the resurrected tribal system. We live in a world today where people are fascinated, and rightfully so, with the nation or the entity we know as Israel. The nation has an amazing story. After 2,000 years of nomadic life, after 2,000 years of being disbursed, in 1917 the Balfour Declaration said they could go back to their homeland. In 1948 the Israelites received their independence as a separate country and were recognized by the world at large. In 1967 they took possession of what we now know as Jerusalem. It is amazing that we live in a society and a world where everybody wants to claim that Jerusalem does not really belong to the nation of Israel. The Bible clearly teaches that Jerusalem belongs to the nation of Israel.

So, the big debate becomes this: what really makes Israel, Israel? Is it just a piece of dirt? That is important. But, is it the fact that they possess the holiest city on earth known as Jerusalem? What is it that really makes Israel, Israel? I think you have to go back to the father of the Israelites, Abraham. Remember Abraham, Isaac and Jacob? It was Jacob who would father these tribes, the tribal system of Israel that was prominent in the Old Testament and resurfaces in Revelation 7. The "physical father" of the Israelites was Jacob, who was renamed Israel. The nation of Israel, in totality, is these twelve tribes.

An interesting event has occurred over the last 2,000 years. You see, you can ask even the most faithful Jewish people which tribe they belong to but they do not know the answer. Now, that is nothing negative toward them. The importance here is that in the Book of Revelation, in the midst of the tribulation, somehow, some way (and I have a lot of theories about this, but I will have to write them in another book!) the identity of these twelve tribes will resurface and be resurrected. Revelation chapter 7 clearly teaches that twelve thousand of each of the twelve tribes are sent out.

The 144,000 are the resurrection of the tribal order but also a realization of Romans 11:25-26. In several chapters prior to Romans 11, the Apostle Paul has been dealing with the fact that even though God called Israel, the tribal system, that we Gentiles could still be saved through Jesus Christ.

Romans 11:25-27 says:

> For I would not, brethren, that you should be ignorant of this mystery, lest you should be wise in your own conceits; that blindness in part is happened to Israel, until the fullness of the Gentiles be come in. And so all Israel shall be saved: as it is written, There shall come out of Sion the Deliverer, and shall turn away ungodliness from Jacob: For this is my covenant unto them, when I shall take away their sins.

I do not believe this passage of scripture teaches that everyone of Jewish descent has a free pass into heaven. What it does teach is that the Lord worked through the Jewish people, the Israelites, throughout the Old Testament. There was, as a whole, a rejection of Jesus. When that Priest made the statement, "May His blood be on us and our children," how much more of a rejection can you get? When you study the book of Acts in the New Testament, you see early in the stages of the church that it was not necessarily the Jewish people as a whole that received the message of Jesus as it was the Gentiles. The Bible says "until the fullness of the *Gentiles* (italics mine) come in and then. . ."

Do you know there are over 250 references in the Book of Revelation to the Old Testament? Almost every illustration given that is of a positive nature goes back to the Old Testament and the history of the Israelite people, the Jewish people. The reason this is significant is that the Bible says all Israel shall be saved. Who is Israel? Jacob; the twelve tribes. What do you have in Revelation 7? You have a very distinct picture of each one of these tribes. I do not believe it is saying only twelve thousand of every tribe "was saved." Instead, I think, of these particular tribes, twelve thousand specific, distinct individuals were set aside for a very specific purpose.

So, we understand that the 144,000 is a distinct and different group. The 144,000 is the resurrection of the tribal system and the realization that Romans 11:25-26 will come to fruition. The time of the Gentiles (that includes most of us) will fade away and once again God will work through the tribes of the Jewish people.

WHEN WILL THE 144,000 BECOME PROMINENT?

A Unique Time

Today people everywhere claim to be the 144,000. Understand that the 144,000 will appear during a very unique time in history. In the Book of Revelation there is a seven year period that we call the great tribulation. Revelation 7:14 says the 144,000 are they which came out of the great tribulation. Revelation makes it very specific that the group is uniquely confined to the time period of the great tribulation. What that means is that the 144,000 appears during the great tribulation, not during our present, current day as many would propagate today.

An Undefined Time

There are several chapters in the Book of Revelation that do not necessarily, seamlessly flow chronologically; these chapters are parenthetical. Revelation chapter 7, Revelation chapter 10, and Revelation chapter 14 are examples of parenthetical chapters. Parenthetically, the Lord takes us out of the current time frame, He gives us a background kind of picture, and then He picks right back up again in the current time frame. We are not told if the 144,000 are revealed in the second year of the tribulation or the third year of the tribulation. We are really not told when this comes to fruition.

We have a hint of when in the tribulation, the 144,000 comes on the scene because the Bible says that one of the tribes is the Levi tribe. Revelation chapter 11 discusses the measuring of the temple and the sacrifices that are to be made. In that sacrificial system and all that will take place at a rampant rate, why would the 144,000 be set aside in this capacity? During the abomination of desolations the character known as the Antichrist comes in and falsely worships in that temple ground. He decimates and desolates, and then later the Israelite people run for their lives. Quite possibly the time period could be toward the end of the tribulation. But, to be honest with you, the time period is really undefined. We just do not know at what stage or in what part the 144,000 are specifically revealed; however, it is very clear that the 144,000 are revealed during the tribulation in a very unique time period.

WHY IS THERE 144,000?

What is so significant about this group of people that everybody, it seems like, wants to be a part of? Everybody wants to claim that the 144,000 is their group. We know the 144,000 is different; we know they are distinct. We know they are a resurrected tribal system; we know that it is a restoration of Romans 11. We know that it happens in the tribulation, so why the 144,000?

The purpose of Revelation is to share the gospel with all.

222

The first reason is this: the 144,000 is a fulfillment of the promise of God. In Genesis 12 God comes to a man by the name of Abram (at the time his name was not yet Abraham). He is far along in his age; his wife is far along in her age. God calls Abram out of Ur of the Chaldees. According to Hebrews 11, he goes to a land that he knew not of. Basically, Abram goes from the area of what we would call northern Iraq down to the area we would consider Saudi Arabia.

In Genesis 15, he looks up in the sky and the Lord says, "How many stars do you see?"

Abram says, "I can't number them."

The Lord says, "And so shall your descendents be. Do you believe?"

Abram says, "I believe."

We know the story—even through a few bumps and through some things that were not picture perfect, Isaac is born, Abraham's descendent. Genesis 22 tells us that Isaac is taken up on Mount Moriah and offered for a sacrifice; however, the Lord spares him. Isaac then fathers Jacob, the twelve tribes. That is the Old Testament in a nutshell.

But, one of the promises to Abraham, Isaac and Jacob that extends throughout the Old Testament is that all nations would know the living true God through their lineage. Notice what happens in Revelation 7:9, "After this I beheld, and, lo, a great multitude, which no man could number, of all nations, and kindreds, and people, and tongues." Now I'm not a linguistics expert, but "after this" cannot be "before that." Think about that for a moment. Understand that the promise that was given to Abraham, that all nations would know the living true God through his seed and through his descendents, is coming true. It is because of these 144,000; it is because of these distinct, different people going into all of the world that all nations, all kindreds, all people and all tongues would know the living true God. So, the 144,000 is the fulfillment of the promise of God.

But I think the most important thing Revelation chapter 7 reveals is a clear process of the gospel. (By the way, the term gospel means good news.)

To be quite honest with you, there are a lot of groups today who claim to be a part of the 144,000. They hand out magazines; they knock on doors. Oftentimes I get into discussions with people who ask why we are not more like that? Why do Christians not show more zeal and zealousness? Every group who has ever claimed or who currently claim to be a part of the 144,000 may have their identity wrong, but they have their actions right. In this passage of Revelation 7 we see the process of the gospel. The purpose for this group is not to say, "We are the special ones." The purpose is not to go hide in a cave and say, "Let's wait this thing out." No, this group says, "The time is short. We have got to 'get after it.' We will waste no expense. We will waste no time. We will make sure that everyone we come across—every person, every tribe, every tongue—will hear the gospel."

We have studied the book of Revelation. We have talked about the Antichrist. We have talked about Jesus Christ. We have talked about the millennium. Has studying these concepts made you want to dig a cave, hide, and think, "Oh no, the sky is falling. This stuff is horrible. I do not even want to think about these things"? That is one of the problems we face when we study the Book of Revelation—it causes us to get a very inward-focused mentality. We hear that all of these horrible things are going to happen. Some people believe that they have to buy and stockpile everything. Others think they have to have military meals ready to eat for the next twelve years, dig a cave that is bunker-proof and just hide out. I believe, based on Revelation 7 (and the role of 144,000) that we understand the book of Revelation, not when it causes us to fear and to go dig a cave, but when it inspires us, at all cost and all expense, to go forth and make sure that everyone hears the gospel of Jesus Christ. That is the purpose of Revelation. The very first three verses of Revelation remind us that the time is at hand; it says the time is short. As you continue to study the Book of Revelation, if you ever find yourself becoming secluded and a recluse in your mind, you have missed the message. In the midst of studying the great tribulation, the Antichrist, the abomination of desolations, these 144,000—in the midst of examining all these things—make sure that you remember what the Bible says in Revelation 7:9, "after this all nations, all kindreds, all people and all tongues." The purpose of Revelation is to share the gospel with all.

You may ask, "How do we share the gospel with all?" Missions. Let me 225 define missions. There are signs at the exit of our campus that read, "You are now entering the mission field." Our church has the privilege to support and to be a part of international and domestic mission endeavors. But I want to be clear, missions is not just about going overseas; missions is about sharing the gospel with your neighbor who does not know Jesus. Missions is about telling your coworker the truth about Jesus. Missions is about sharing the gospel message with the school down the street. Missions is showing Christ to the restaurant waitress. Understand that just because we talk about another country, just because we talk about an incredible trip, do not classify that as being all that missions is about. According to Revelation, the 144,000 did not just go to those across the ocean. They went to all nations, all kindreds, all people, and all tongues. I am of a belief that when you understand Revelation you begin to have a passion for missions; you begin to have a passion to give more to missions and to go on more missions—whether that is a trip overseas to share the gospel or a trip to your next door neighbor to give them food while they are sick and to share the gospel. This is why we are who we are: changing the world, starting here.

CPSIA information can be obtained at www.ICGtesting.com
Printed in the USA
LVOW060957181111

255539LV00004B/3/P